up every morning, run to the calendar and wait for my mom. We never had enough paper, so when mom would rip each day's page off the calendar, I'd use it to draw. One day of each month was marked by an extra-large page, which meant a jumbo-sized drawing!

I have a series in *Jump* getting a graphic novel release. But I don't take credit for that—I chalk it up to the power of manga. To that five-year-old with nothing more than calendar pages to draw on, *Jump* shone bright as a beacon telling me that I too could become a mangaka someday.

RIICHIRO INAGAKI

I may be the writer, but I can't do any of this on my own. This series is the product of a lot of hard work from a lot of people.

Senku starts gathering his own group of friends in this volume, and with their help, he's able to create all sorts of things.

The picture above is my attempt to make a certain one of those things. It tasted, let's just say... interesting!

Boichi is a Korean-born artist currently living and working in Japan. His previous works include *Sun-Ken Rock* and *Terra Formars Asimov.*

Riichiro Inagaki is a Japanese manga writer from Tokyo. He is the writer for the sports manga series *Eyeshield 21*, which was serialized in *Weekly Shonen Jump.*

Dr. STONE

3

SHONEN JUMP Manga Edition

Story **RIICHIRO INAGAKI**
Art **BOICHI**

Translation/**CALEB COOK**
Touch-Up Art & Lettering/**STEPHEN DUTRO**
Design/**JULIAN [JR] ROBINSON**
Editor/**JOHN BAE**
Science Consultant/**KURARE**

Consulted Works:

- Asari, Yoshito, *Uchu e Ikitakute Ekitainenryo Rocket wo DIY Shite Mita (Gakken Rigaku Sensho), Gakken Plus*, 2013
- Dartnell, Lewis, *The Knowledge: How to Rebuild Civilization in the Aftermath of a Cataclysm*, translated by Erika Togo, Kawade Shobo Shinsha, 2015
- Davies, Barry, *The Complete SAS Survival Manual*, translated by Yoshito Takigawa, Toyo Shorin, 2001
- Kazama, Rinpei, *Shinboken Techo (Definitive Edition)*, Shufu to Seikatsu Sha, 2016
- McNab, Chris, *Special Forces Survival Guide*, translated by Atsuko Sumi, Hara Shobo, 2016
- Olsen, Larry Dean, *Outdoor Survival Skills*, translated by Katsuji Tani, A&F, 2014
- Weisman, Alan, *The World Without Us*, translated by Shinobu Onizawa, Hayakawa Publishing, 2009
- Wiseman, John, *SAS Survival Handbook, Revised Edition*, translated by Kazuhiro Takahashi and Hitoshi Tomokiyo, Namiki Shobo, 2009

Printed in the U.S.A.

Published by VIZ Media, LLC
P.O. Box 77010
San Francisco, CA 94107

10 9 8 7 6 5 4 3 2 1
First printing, January 2019

viz.com

shonenjump.com

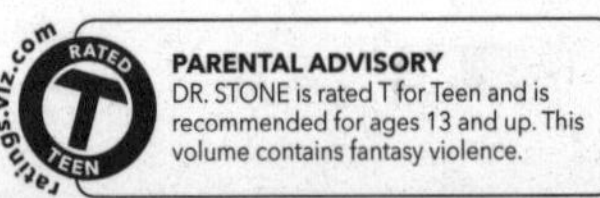

3

TWO MILLION YEARS OF BEING

Dr.STONE

STORY **RIICHIRO INAGAKI**
ART **BOICHI**

CHARACTERS
KOHAKU
SENKU
E=mc²
The first person Senku encounters in the stone world who is not from his high school. She's strong as an ox and quite the fighter, but she sounds a bit old-fashioned at times.
A young man with a passion for science. With belief in the power of science and armed with prodigious knowledge, he's crafted what he needs to survive in this brave new Stone World. His catchphrase is "Get excited!"

STORY

Every human on Earth is turned to stone by a mysterious phenomenon, including high school student Taiju. Nearly 3,700 years later, Taiju awakens and finds his friend Senku, who revived a bit earlier. Together, they vow to restore civilization!

Tsukasa takes Yuzuriha hostage in an attempt to force Senku to give up on science. Negotiations break down and end with Tsukasa delivering a death blow to Senku. While desperately trying to bring Senku back, Taiju and Yuzuriha notice a leftover stone fragment on his neck. Just a little bit of revival fluid is all they need to save their scientist friend!

After their close call, the group decides to split up. Taiju and Yuzuriha go off to spy on Tsukasa while keeping him in the dark about Senku's miraculous survival. Meanwhile, Senku sets out to establish a kingdom of science. He starts by finding the person who sent up the smoke signals—a girl named Kohaku!

CONTENTS

3
TWO MILLION YEARS OF BEING

Z=17: Nasty Looks

THUD
MY NAME IS KOHAKU.
AND I DO BELIEVE...
...I'VE FALLEN FOR YOU QUITE HARD.
...
SHEESH...
ANNOYING CRAP LIKE THAT MAKES ME WANNA CURL UP AND DIE.

I MEAN, REALLY? YOU'VE GOT A CRUSH ON ME NOW? IN AN EMERGENCY LIKE THIS...?
!!!
I'M NOT SAYING THAT AT ALL!

I'M SAYING I'LL COOPERATE WITH YOU, BECAUSE I LIKE YOU!!
OH. I APPRECIATE IT.
A BRAIN CLOUDED BY LOVE IS THE MOST IRRATIONAL KIND. IT LEADS TO NOTHING BUT TROUBLE.

...
SO YOU NEW HUMANS SLEEP WITH BLADES IN HAND?
IT'S PRETTY OBVIOUS I DON'T HAVE "LOVE" ON THE BRAIN, RIGHT?

HAH! I MAY BE CURIOUS ABOUT YOUR WAYS, BUT THAT DOESN'T MEAN I TRUST YOU.
THIS IS JUST A HABIT FROM HAVING HAD TO PROTECT MYSELF MY ENTIRE LIFE. DON'T LET IT GET TO YOU.
I AIN'T SO BRAVE TO SUDDENLY ATTACK A LIONESS LIKE YOU. SO DON'T WASTE ANOTHER 0.1 SECONDS AND GET TO SLEEP ALREADY.
A LIONESS ?!
THAT'S MEAN!
YOU MAY LIVE LIKE A GENTLEMAN, BUT YOUR SUPER-FILTHY MOUTH TELLS A DIFFERENT STORY.
MY BLADE MAY FIND THAT SHARP TONGUE OF YOURS BEFORE EITHER OF US KNOWS IT...

THAT LONG-HAIRED MAN...
YOU'RE FIGHTING HIM?
I WOULD BE HAPPY TO HELP!
I'M NOT ONE TO RETREAT IN DISGRACE, YOU KNOW.

YEP. THAT'S WHY I'M BUILDING A KINGDOM OF SCIENCE.
SCIENCE? YOU MEAN YOUR SORCERY?
BUT FIRST...
I NEED MANPOWER!
THEN YOU SHOULD COME WITH ME.
I'LL BE RETURNING HOME AFTER FETCHING SOME HOT SPRING WATER.

HOT SPRING WATER?

SPLISH

THIS WILL MAKE A FINE HOT BATH ONCE I CARRY IT BACK.
SPLASH
PERFECT FOR REJUVENATION.

BUT YOU'RE TEN BILLION PERCENT HEALTHY.
WHY WOULD A VIGOROUS LIONESS LIKE YOU NEED REJUVENATION?
I AM NO LIONESS!
AND IT'S FOR MY OLDER SISTER!!

I SWEAR...
SHE'S SUCH A NUISANCE.
THAT SISTER OF MINE ONLY SLOWS ME DOWN.
SHE'S BEEN SICK LATELY...
IF I COULD TAKE HER PLACE...
...AND GIVE HER THIS HEALTHY BODY OF MINE, I WOULD.
...

THAT POT ONLY HOLDS ABOUT 50 LITERS.
NOT EXACTLY ENOUGH FOR A FULL-BLOWN BATH.
HOW MANY TIMES HAVE YOU GONE BACK AND FORTH...
...CARRYING THAT BIG, HEAVY THING...
...DAY...
...AFTER DAY?

HAH! IT SERVES AS MY DAILY TRAINING.
THE WATER IS JUST HEAVY ENOUGH FOR THAT.
IT HELPS STRENGTHEN MY BODY, SO...
...I SUPPOSE I HAVE TO THANK MY TROUBLESOME SISTER FOR THAT.

WOBBLE
!

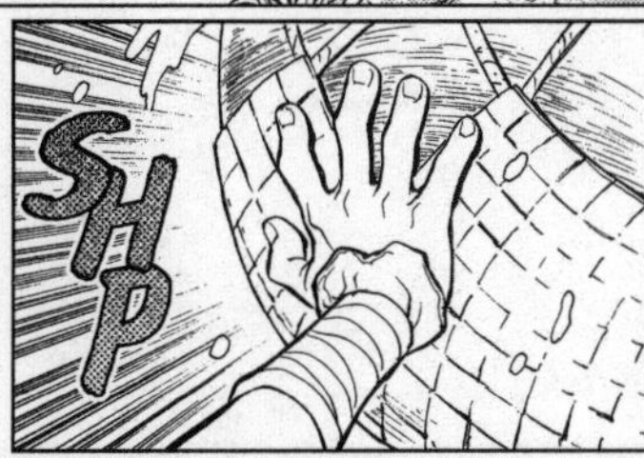
SHP

YOU'RE STILL NOT TOTALLY HEALED FROM EARLIER, HUH?
I'LL BE IN A REAL PINCH IF YOU OVERDO IT AND KICK THE BUCKET.
LEMME LEND YOU A HAND.

SENKU...

TALK ABOUT OVER-DOING IT.
AM I THE ONLY ONE IN THIS STONE WORLD WHO'S NOT A GORILLA?
KOHAKU, TSUKASA, TAIJU...

GORILLA?! GO BACK TO LIONESS! I PREFER THAT!
YOU'RE MISSING MY POINT...

CLATTERCLATTER

CLATTER
CLATTER
CLATTER

AMAZING, BUILDING SUCH A USEFUL CONTRAPTION SO QUICKLY!
SO QUICKLY?
IT'S ONLY BECAUSE I HAD THE PERFECT SET OF MATERIALS FROM THE PULLEYS YESTERDAY.
PROGRESS GIVES RISE TO FURTHER PROGRESS.
AND PRACTICAL APPLICATION OF THAT PROGRESS IS AT THE CORE OF SCIENCE!
WE'RE HERE...
SENKU!!

WEL-
COME...
...TO MY
VILLAGE!

HOW MANY PEOPLE LIVE HERE...?
I FORGET HOW MANY CHILDREN AND ELDERS THERE ARE, BUT THEM ASIDE...
...WE HAVE EXACTLY...
...40!

Carbo
Hagane
Genbu
Kohaku
Beryl
Argo
Magma
Ruri
Natri
Tetsuken
Mantle
Kokuyo
Alumi
Kinro
Shirogane
Jasper
Kaseki
Ginro
Turquoise

Alabaster
Sho
Suika
Titan
Dia
Sango
Unmo
Suzu
Ruby
Azura
Chrome
Sagan
Sapphire
Kujaku
Shovel
En
Garnet
Chalk
Namari
Ganen

PROBABLY NEITHER KOHAKU NOR THE OTHERS...
...KNOW SQUAT ABOUT MODERN CIVILIZATION.

?

WHICH MEANS THIS SETTLEMENT...
...IS MADE UP OF THE DESCENDANTS OF THOSE REVIVED FROM STONE!!

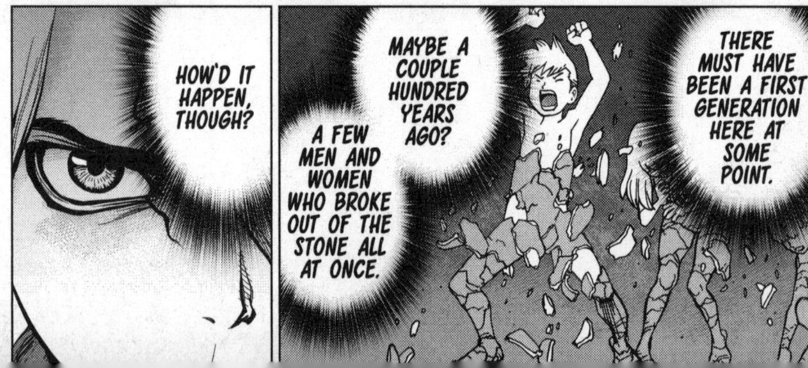
THERE MUST HAVE BEEN A FIRST GENERATION HERE AT SOME POINT.
MAYBE A COUPLE HUNDRED YEARS AGO?
A FEW MEN AND WOMEN WHO BROKE OUT OF THE STONE ALL AT ONCE.
HOW'D IT HAPPEN, THOUGH?

WAS THERE A MAN OF SCIENCE, LIKE ME, WHO CREATED A REVIVAL FLUID?
BUT THEN YOU'D EXPECT HIS DESCEN-DANTS...
...WOULD KNOW ABOUT THE FLUID, AND ABOUT THE POWER OF SCIENCE.
WHERE'D THESE PEOPLE COME FROM?
THIS WHOLE VILLAGE...??
TMP
TMP

ZOOSH

WHAP
WHAP
!!
NO VIOLENCE, KINRO, GINRO!
I'M ALIVE THANKS TO THIS MAN!!

SORRY 'BOUT THAT, KOHAKU.
BUT NO CAN DO.
NO OUTSIDERS ALLOWED. YOU KNOW THAT.
THE CHIEF'LL BE MAD.
SO THERE'RE HUMANS OUT THERE BESIDES US!
I'VE NEVER SEEN ONE BEFORE.
THERE'S NOTHING TO ARGUE ABOUT.
RULES...
...ARE RULES.

"NO HUMANS LIVE BEYOND OUR BORDERS."
ANY OUTSIDERS HAFTA BE CRIMINALS WE KICKED OUT IN THE PAST.
HE CANNOT STAY HERE.
WHETHER HE'S YOUR SAVIOR OR NOT, THE DETAILS DON'T MATTER.

YOU LEAVE ME NO CHOICE.

RIGHT HERE. RIGHT NOW.
FIGHT ME!
TWO-ON-ONE, THOUGH! THE ADVANTAGE IS YOURS, SO I'M IN BIIIIG TROUBLE!

SHUDDER
...

HEH HEH HEH...
I'VE WALKED INTO A POWDER KEG, HUH?
DON'T GIMME THOSE NASTY LOOKS, FELLAS.

SORCERY?!

FWOO

HAH!!
ZOOSH

SQUISH
POP
HALT
HOW MYSTERIOUS...
FLYING JEWELS...?!

WHUT?!
THEY'RE THAT PRIMITIVE, HUH?

HEH HEH HEH... PERFECT. THEY'LL ALL BE MINE.
I'LL HAVE THE POWER OF SCIENCE AND 40 PEOPLE TO BOOT...
...ONCE I RECRUIT THIS BUNCH TO MY CAUSE.
$E=mc^2$
GET EXCITED!!
I DON'T LIKE THAT NASTY LOOK.
YOU BETTER WATCH YOURSELF...
ANYHOW! FIRST...
...YOU'LL NEED TO RECRUIT CHROME.
WHOZZAT?
HEH HEH HEH... A MAN I THINK YOU'LL FIND USEFUL. WHAT'S MORE, HE'S...
...THE MOST EASYGOING OF US ALL!

Kinro and Ginro are brothers, right? Who are their parents?

R.M. from Fukuoka Prefecture SEARCH

This concerns familial relations in the village, right? As some connections may be yet unknown, ongoing analysis is underway!

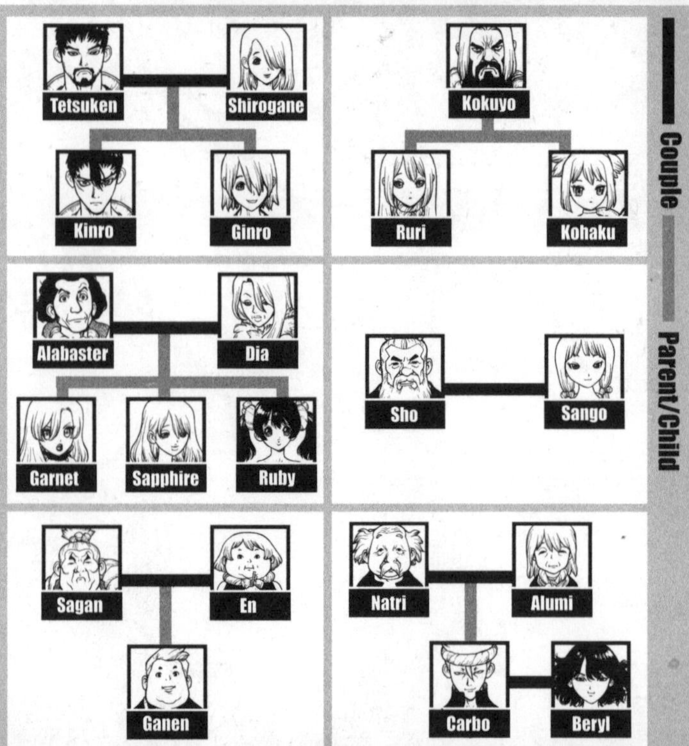

Z=18: Sorcery Showdown
FWOO
BWONG
THESE JEWELS REFUSE TO BE DEFEATED.
STABBING THEM ONLY MAKES MORE!
THERE'S NO CHOICE!
I MUST USE MY SECRET TECHNIQUE!
ZOOSH

HEYYY! SOMEONE'S USING SORCERY OVER HERE!
CHROME !!
IT'S SOMEONE ELSE'S PROB-LEM!!
SECRET TECHNIQUE...
HEY!
DON'T BE SCARED, GINRO.
I'M ALREADY HERE!
TOMP
HEY! I'M CHROME.
AND I'VE GOT ONE BAAAD HEAD ON MY SHOULDERS!
I SAW THESE FROM THE COAST AND CAME RUNNING!
BECAUSE THAT'S WHAT I DO!

I'M A GENIUS...
...SORCERER !!
OH YEAH? WELL I'M SENKU, SCIENCE USER.
HAH! SPEAK OF THE DEVIL.
THIS SAVES US THE TROUBLE OF TRYING TO FIND HIM.

DON'T GET SCARED BY PETTY MAGIC LIKE THIS, KINRO, GINRO!
Huh?
Huh?

!

THESE THINGS?
POP
I CAN MAKE AS MANY AS I WANT FROM CHARCOAL LYE!!
POP

WE WEREN'T SCARED.
BUT ONLY A FOOL LETS DOWN HIS GUARD IN THE FACE OF THE UNKNOWN.
I WAS ACTUALLY SCARED. YUP.

WHY DID YOU COME, ANYWAY?
I'D RATHER NOT RELY ON YOUR DUBIOUS SORCERY, CHROME!
YOUR CHOICE. I DON'T CARE.

BUT I WON'T BE UPSTAGED!
SORCERY IS MY DOMAIN!
SO BACK OFF!!

A SORCERY SHOWDOWN?!
TMP
TMP
TMP
THEY'LL PROBABLY END UP DESTROYING THE WHOLE VILLAGE!!
THE CHIEF'S NOT GONNA LIKE THIS ONE BIT!

BOOM
SENKU VS CHROME
THINGS COULD GET HAIRY FOR THE VILLAGERS IF WE FIGHT HERE, AND WE CAN'T HAVE THAT.
LET'S PICK A DIFFERENT LOCATION!

OH! HOLD ON!
JUST WAIT RIGHT HERE!!
ZOOM
BWUMP
...?
HE RAN OFF TO GET SOMETHING?
SO, CHANGING BATTLE-FIELDS...
...WAS JUST SO HE COULD RETRIEVE HIS TOOLS...
KRAKL KRAKL
KRAKL
BEHOLD!
MY BAAAD SORCERY!

RAINBOW BRIDGE!
WATCH AS I...
...MANIPU-LATE FIRE!!
FWOOSH

THE FLAMES ...
... TURNED YELLOW!

FWOOOM
HOW?!

BWOOOM
ANOTHER CHANGE!
BLUE ... NO, GREEN ?!

BWOOOSH
PURPLE !!

AMAZING!
...
WHAT SORCERY !!
...
RAINBOW BRIDGE? WHAT A BUNCHA CRAP. IT'S JUST A SERIES OF FLAME REACTIONS.
SALT.
COPPER.
SULFUR.
YOU TOSSED THOSE IN, IN THAT ORDER.

WHERE'D YOU GET THE COPPER? COPPER SULFATE, I'M GUESSING?
YOU WOULDN'T KNOW TO CALL IT THAT, PROBABLY.
YOU SNATCHED SOME BLUE CRYSTALS OUT OF A CAVE, RIGHT?

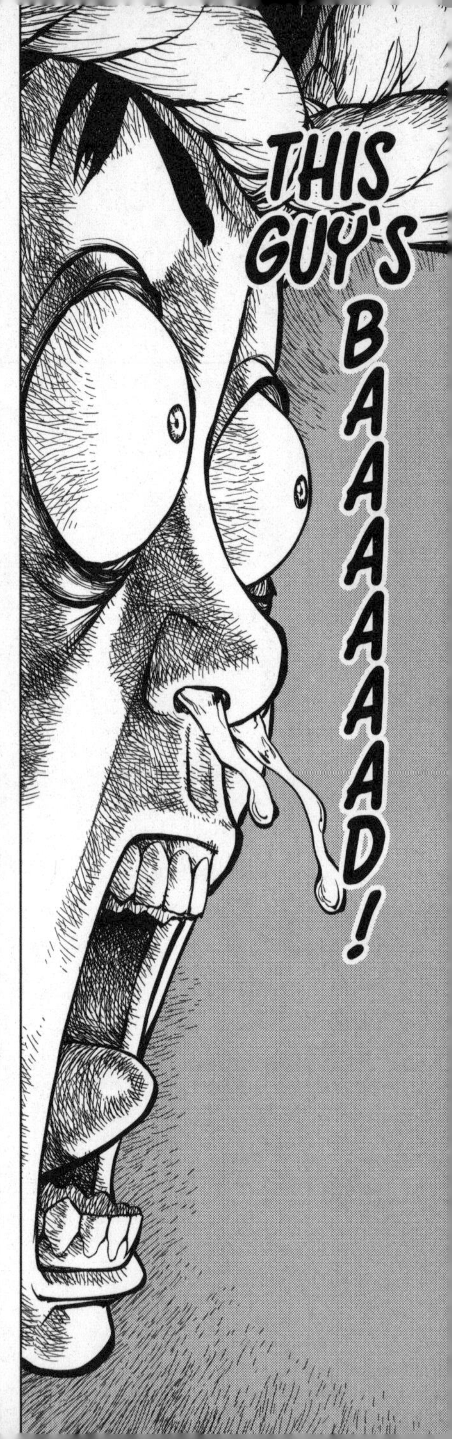
THIS GUY'S BAAAAAAAD!

WHO IS HE?!
HE KNEW ABOUT THE BLUE CRYSTALS?
I CAN'T DEAL WITH MIND-READING SORCERY. THAT'S BAAAD NEWS.
WHO KNEW SORCERY LIKE THAT EXISTED? THE NATURAL WORLD IS BAAAD!

KHAHA HAHA
Eek! Scary. I'm running away now.
I have underestimated you. Please make me your apprentice!
I WAS SURE IT'D TURN OUT ONE OF THESE TWO WAYS, BUT HE'S A BADDER DUDE THAN THAT.
EVEN WITH THE APPRENTICE OPTION, I WAS READY TO START WORRYING ABOUT HOW TO HANDLE THAT BURDEN. THIS IS BAD...

OH, WELL DONE! MY SORCERY WAS, WELL...
...YOU BETTER NOT BE THINKING IT WAS JUST A BIG BLUFF!
WE DIDN'T SAY ANYTHING.

HANG ON. I'LL BE RIGHT BACK...
...WITH A BAAAD THING THAT'LL REALLY PUT THE HURT ON YOU!
BWUMP
IT'S SERIOUSLY GONNA BE BAD THIS TIME!!
RUB
RUB
RUB

RUB
RUB
RUB
RUB
RUB
RUB

HAHH!
HAHH!
HAHH!
WAHH! THAT HURT!
WHAT THE HECK IS THAT ATTACK?!
KZZT

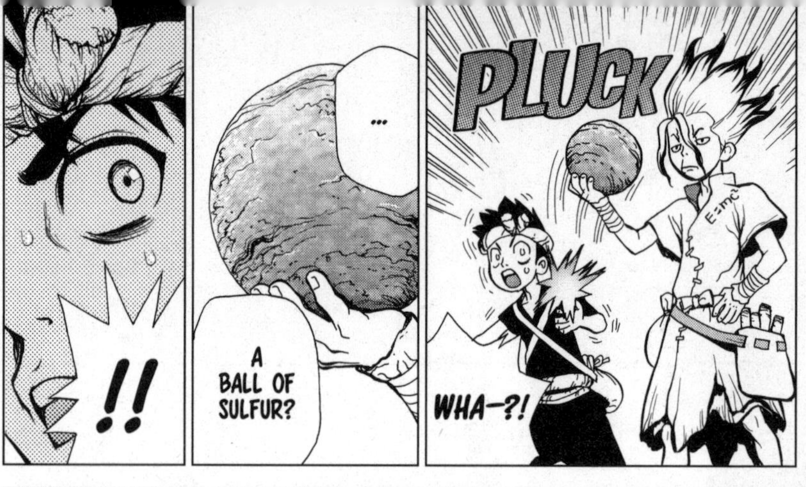
PLUCK
WHA-?!
...
A BALL OF SULFUR?
!!

THAT SULFUR YOU TOSSED INTO THE FIRE EARLIER...
YOU MUST'VE PUT IT IN A POT, MELTED IT DOWN.
AFTER IT COOLED DOWN AND HARDENED, YOU CHIPPED OFF THE POT.
NEAT WAY OF GOING ABOUT IT!
I'M GETTING EXCITED ABOUT YOU, CHROME!

DISCHARGING STATIC ELECTRICITY FROM BALLS OF SULFUR...
...DIDN'T COME ABOUT UNTIL THE 17TH CENTURY.
HEH HEH HEH... BUT WHY RUB WITH YOUR HANDS WHEN LEATHER WILL PRODUCE TEN BILLION TIMES MORE POWER?

MY SCIENCE FLAG!
KERZZAP
BAAAAD!!
SENKU'S HAIR IS ALL STANDING UP!
EVEN THOUGH IT WAS ALREADY STANDING UP BEFORE.

WHAT IS THIS? BABY'S FIRST SCIENCE EXPERI-MENTS?
YOU PRIMITIVE BUNCH OF...
$E=mc^2$

CHROME.
DID YOU THINK UP ALL THIS STUFF...
...ON YOUR OWN, IN THIS PRIMITIVE VILLAGE?

ALL THE MINERALS AND RAW SCIENTIFIC MATERIALS...
IN THAT STOREHOUSE...
DID YOU COLLECT THEM ALL YOURSELF?

YEAH, I DID! SORRY!
SO GIVE THAT BACK...

KIDS COLLECT ALL SORTS OF THINGS, RIGHT?
I FOUND THEM, SMASHED THEM, MIXED THEM, BURNED THEM...
AND WHEN SOMETHING BAAAD HAPPENS, THAT'S SORCERY!
THAT'S ALL I'VE BEEN DOING, I SWEAR!!
HEH HEH HEH... YOU SEE THAT, TSUKASA?
YOU CAN KILL ME. YOU CAN KILL WHOEVER YOU WANT.

BUT TRY AS YOU MIGHT TO RESET SCIENCE...
WE SMOOTH AND SHINY MONKEYS...
...HAVE AMONG US BAAAD BLOCKHEADS LIKE THIS ONE WHO'LL EXPERIMENT WITH EVERY-THING.
AND THEY'LL ALWAYS BE THERE TO REVIVE...
...A SCIENTIFIC CIVILIZATION!

$E=mc^2$

TMP
$E=mc^2$

CHROME. KEEP THIS UP, AND THERE'S A TEN BILLION PERCENT CHANCE...
...THAT YOU'LL BE ONE OF THE ONES TSUKASA IS OUT TO SLAUGHTER.
E=mc²
YOU'VE GOT NO CHOICE BUT TO JOIN ME AND MY KINGDOM OF SCIENCE!
?

HEH HEH HEH... AND THE KINGDOM CAN'T WAIT TO GET ITS HANDS ON THIS SCIENCE STOREHOUSE OF YOURS.
NO WAY, YOU JERK. GET DOWN FROM THERE!
I LOOK LIKE SUCH A FOOL.
I'D RATHER DIE THAN BACK DOWN FROM THIS BATTLE.
ONE MORE CONTEST. JUST YOU AND ME!

IF YOU LOSE, YOU'LL BOW DOWN TO ME AND LEAVE OUR VILLAGE FOR GOOD!
IF YOU WIN, IT'S ALL YOURS...
ME AND MY STORE-HOUSE!!

CONTEST?
GET READY FOR SOME BAAAD SKILLS.
NO ONE'S EVER MATCHED ME WHEN IT COMES TO THIS!

BA M
FACE ME IN A BATTLE...
...IN THE ART OF ADDING!!
I HAVE A FEELING THAT SENKU IS EVEN MORE UNMATCHED THERE.

Science storehouse and Chrome—acquired!!

If X people catch Y fish each, how many fish are caught, total?
Getting *multiple* headaches just trying to figure out this math.
Get it?! I call it *multiplication!!*

Side Story
Chrome vs. Senku
Arithme-Battle!!
YOU READY? CUZ I'VE GOT SOME BAAAAD MATH FOR YOU.
TIME FOR AN ARITHME-BATTLE!!
8×8=?
VMOOM

POOF
64
CRUD... SURE, SENKU GOT IT, BUT...
EVEN YOU, KOHAKU?
WELL, WHEN WATCHING A SCHOOL OF FISH...
...IT'S AN EASY WAY TO ESTIMATE HOW MANY THERE ARE.
8
8
Eyesight: 20/1.8
OH YEAH? FINE THEN!
KRAKL
TAKE THIS!!

83x87
=?
HUMMM
FLING
HOW ON EARTH COULD ANYONE KNOW THAT?!
7221
FWOO

LISTEN, CHROME. WHAT YOU'RE TRYING TO SHOW OFF IS A QUICK-SOLVE METHOD, RIGHT?
8
3
SAME
ADD UP TO 10
8
7
ADD UP THE DIGITS IN THE ONES PLACES TO GET TEN.
THIS TRICK ONLY WORKS WHEN THE TENS PLACES HAVE THE SAME DIGIT, THOUGH.
8 × 8 9 3 × 7
EIGHT BUMPS UP TO NINE, THEN JUST MULTIPLY
MULTIPLY THE ONES PLACES
Answer
72 21
Could always just brute force it anyway.
WHAT POSSIBLE PURPOSE...
...COULD THIS SO-CALLED ARITHMETIC SERVE IN BATTLE?
Y-YOU COULD USE IT FOR ANALYZING POWER LEVELS!
COULD BE USEFUL FOR ASSIGNING FIGHTERS IN TEAM BOUTS.
THROWING MODESTY TO THE WIND, I'D SAY MY POWER LEVEL...
...IS ABOUT 1,000.

KINRO IS 500.
GINRO IS 100.
CHROME IS 5.
I'M NOT THAT WEAK!!
AND SENKU IS 3.
HEH HEH HEH... WITHOUT MY SCIENCE? SURE.

PERHAPS, BUT DON'T UNDERESTIMATE ME.
APOLOGIES. IF YOU WISH...
...WE COULD ALL SPAR RIGHT HERE AND NOW!
WHAT IS THIS, SOME IMPOSSIBLE GAME?!

HEH HEH... I'VE GOT A GREAT IDEA.
HOW ABOUT THE FOUR OF US TEAM UP?
EVEN THE MIGHTY KOHAKU WON'T STAND A CHANCE!
THAT'S NOT COWARDLY. NOT AT ALL...!

LIKE. I. SAID.
500 + 100 + 5 + 3 < 1000.
THAT'S JUST MATH.
FSSHHH
I NOW UNDERSTAND.

How did everyone do in school?

Nien-san and others from Tokyo SEARCH

The villagers do not have anything resembling an educational institution, but were they to start one...I have constructed this diagram of their respective intelligences!

Bad — Grades — Good

Z=19: Two Million Years of Being

RATTLE
GET EXCITED!
A whole bunch of minerals acquired!!

HEH HEH HEH... YOU'VE GATHERED UP SO MUCH STUFF...
SPARKLE
HOW MANY YEARS DID THIS TAKE, CHROME?!
SPARKLE

YEAH, TAKE A LOOK, SENKU. BAAAD, AIN'T IT?
SPARKLE
SPARKLE
SURE, YOU BEAT ME AT SORCERY AND MATH... I WASN'T IN TOP FORM TODAY.
BUT MY COLLECTION HERE CAN'T BE BEAT!!

SURE. BUT IN THE END IT'S STILL JUST...
...A BUNCH OF ROCKS.

MALACHITE.
CHAL-
CANTHITE.
CORUNDUM.
THAT BAAAD ONE'S SUPER HARD!
NOT SEEING A DIFFERENCE.
HOW COULD A COUPLE ROCKS TURN YOU TWO INTO RAGING FANATICS?
OH, HERE WE GO! GALENA!!
SWEET, SWEET LEAD!
CRACK IT AND IT SPARKLES REAL BAAAD!
NOPE. I'LL NEVER UNDERSTAND WHY BOYS TREASURE EVERY LITTLE THING THEY COLLECT.
I USED TO COLLECT INSECTS, ACTUALLY.
BUT NOW I THINK THEY'RE GROSS. WON'T EVEN TOUCH 'EM.

OOOOOH
THERE'S EVEN A PHILOSOPHER'S STONE!
HE CAN DROOL OVER HIS SPOILS OF WAR ALL HE WANTS. I'M DONE.
MY SISTER NEEDS THIS HOT SPRING WATER.

KR
RAK
CINNABAR. COMMONLY KNOWN AS THE PHILOSOPHER'S STONE.
IT EVEN MAKES AN APPEARANCE IN *DRAGON QUEST*.
WE CAN EXTRACT MERCURY BY HEATING IT.
MORE CREEPY SORCERY, HUH?
DO AS YOU LIKE OUTSIDE THE VILLAGE BORDER.
WHAP
BUT TAKE ONE STEP ON THIS BRIDGE, AND I SHALL CUT YOU DOWN.
RULES ARE RULES.
E=mc²
TAKE THE MERCURY...
...AND MELT SOME GOLD DUST INTO IT...
DIP
BREATHE IN THAT SMOKE, AND IT'LL BE THE LAST THING YOU DO.
!!

*KIN MEANS "GOLD" IN JAPANESE.

...
KINRO!
WELL...
NO NEED TO TROUBLE YOURSELVES WITH STRIPPING IT OFF.
HEH HEH HEH... ONE MORE GOOD PUSH AND HE'S OURS!
ANY CHANCE I CAN GET A SILVER SPEAR?
BADUM
BADUM

YOU'RE LIKE ONE OF THOSE MONSTER HUNTER GAMERS...
MONSTER WHAT?
...WHO DOES NOTHING BUT COLLECT RAW MATERIALS.
GREEN GENTIAN...
...HEMERO-CALLIS, COPTIS...
ALL GOOD FOR TRADITIONAL CHINESE HEALING.
THIS IS YOUR MEDICINE, HUH?

YEAH.
THOUGH IT'S KINDA HARD TO SAY IF ANY OF IT WORKS.
I ONLY GATHER UP THE STUFF I'VE ALREADY TESTED ON MYSELF.
I'M COLLECTING EVERYTHING I CAN FIND...
...IN THE HOPES OF HEALING RURI.
THAT'S WHY...
...I TURNED TO SORCERY IN THE FIRST PLACE!!

I'M GRATEFUL TO YOU, KOHAKU...
...FOR ALWAYS BRINGING THIS HEALING SPRING WATER.

ONLY A SINGLE POTFUL TODAY?
DID SOMETHING HAPPEN?
HAH! I JUST HAPPENED TO FALL ASLEEP ON THE ROAD. THAT'S ALL.
HAP-PENED TO...?
KOHAKU. YOU REALLY NEED TO BE MORE MINDFUL SOMETIMES.

JASPER.
TURQUOISE.
COULD YOU LEAVE US FOR A BIT?
I'D LIKE TO SPEAK WITH KOHAKU ALONE.
I'M AFRAID NOT, LADY RURI.
IT'S OUR DUTY TO GUARD OUR SHAMANESS.
BUT KOHAKU IS MY LITTLE SISTER.

PLEASE.
...

KOHAKU!
YOU DUMMY!

THE KNOT BINDING YOUR HAIR HAS CHANGED.
WHAT DID YOU ENCOUNTER...
...TO CAUSE YOUR HAIR TO COME UNDONE?!
KOFF
KOFF
SISTER!!
PLEASE. NO MORE RECKLESSNESS.
I DON'T HAVE LONG, SO DO THIS FOR ME.

SENKU!
DON'T YOU HAVE SOME SORCERY... OR SCIENCE...
...TO SAVE RURI?!

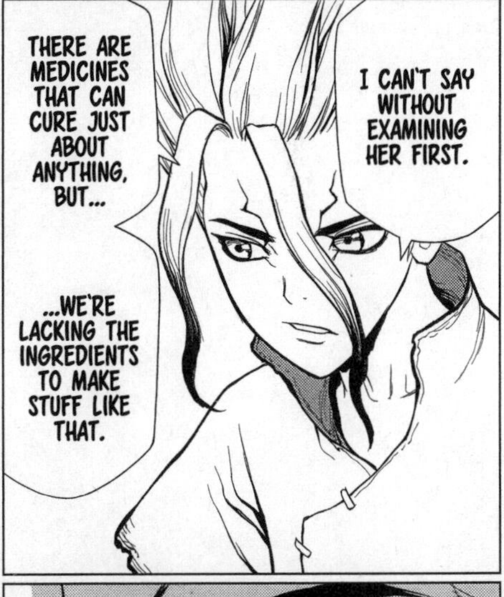
I CAN'T SAY WITHOUT EXAMINING HER FIRST.
THERE ARE MEDICINES THAT CAN CURE JUST ABOUT ANYTHING, BUT...
...WE'RE LACKING THE INGREDIENTS TO MAKE STUFF LIKE THAT.

CHROME. I THINK...
...I'D BETTER TELL YOU EVERYTHING.
ABOUT WHAT HAPPENED 3,700 YEARS AGO.
ABOUT THE WORLD BEFORE THE FALL.

JANET AIRFEIGHT
JANE

ROBO

ARE THOSE TEARS?
ARE YOU HAVING AN EMOTIONAL MOMENT, HERE?
I AIN'T CRYING!!
WAIT. I GUESS I AM!!
SO WHO TURNED EVERYONE TO STONE, HUH?!
LET'S FIND 'EM AND MAKE 'EM PAY!

IT'S JUST SO SAD...
EVERYTHING THAT THE HUMANS BEFORE US BUILT, LITTLE BY LITTLE, OVER MILLIONS OF YEARS...
ALL THAT BAAAD STUFF! THE WHOLE BAAAD SCIENTIFIC CIVILIZATION!!
ALL WIPED OUT IN A FLASH, JUST LIKE THAT!
HOW CAN I NOT FEEL BITTER ABOUT THAT?!
HEH HEH HEH... IT AIN'T WIPED OUT, IDIOT. IT'S ALL STILL HERE.
WHERE?!
HUMANITY'S NOT GOING DOWN THAT EASILY.
TWO MILLION YEARS OF HUMANITY...
IT'S ALL...

... RIGHT HERE!

IT'S IN YOU TOO, BUD.
AM I WRONG...?
...
NO, YOU'RE RIGHT.
OF COURSE I'M RIGHT!

I'LL BUILD THIS KINGDOM OF SCIENCE WITH YOU.
AND MAKE SOME BAAAD MEDICINE THAT'LL CURE ANYTHING.
RURI'S SICKNESS...
...IS GOING DOWN!!

$E=mc^2$
Z=20: Stone Road

AN OUTSIDER??
HMPH ...
DO YOU REMEMBER FROM WAY BACK? WE BANISHED CRIMINALS FROM THE VILLAGE.
THERE HAS TO BE A CONNECTION THERE.
BUT WAIT, HEY, LISTEN, HE'S A YOUNG DUDE!

IF HE STIRS UP TROUBLE, I'LL TAKE HIM OUT!
THEN RURI'LL FALL FOR ME FOR SURE!
OHHH, YEAH.
HEH... IT COULD BE THAT ONE OF THOSE COUNTLESS STONE STATUES WAS REVIVED.
NO WAY...
ALL THAT MATTERS...
...IS WHETHER OR NOT THIS HUNK IS STRONG!
HUH? STRONG? WHO CARES ABOUT JUNK LIKE THAT.
IS HE CUTE?!
YOU'RE TELLING ME THAT THIS OUTSIDER...

...WAS LED STRAIGHT TO US BY KOHAKU?
I'M NOT QUITE SURE YET.
THAT'S RIGHT, CHIEF! IT WAS KOHAKU.
YOU HEARD GINRO TOO, JASPER. NO POINT IN TRYING TO HIDE IT!
MY FOOLISH DAUGHTER!
DOES SHE WANT TO BE DISOWNED?!
...
SHE'S ALWAYS BREAKING THE RULES!!
KOFF
KOFF

HAHH
HAHH
TEACH ME, SENKU! HOW DO WE MAKE THIS CURE?
WE GOTTA KICK RURI'S SICKNESS BACK WHERE IT CAME FROM!!
IF IT'LL HEAL MY SISTER, I'LL DO WHATEVER I CAN TO HELP!
SHAH

SEE THAT?
THAT SLEAZY GLINT IN HIS EYE! HE'S SCHEMING TO SAVE RURI FOR HIS OWN REASONS.
GENTLEMAN? OR SLEAZEBAG? HARD TO SAY.
AT THE VERY LEAST, HE'S RATIONAL ABOUT IT.
Long live science!
Let us join your science kingdom!
RURI
WHAT WE OF THE KINGDOM OF SCIENCE WILL CREATE IS...
SHF
SHF

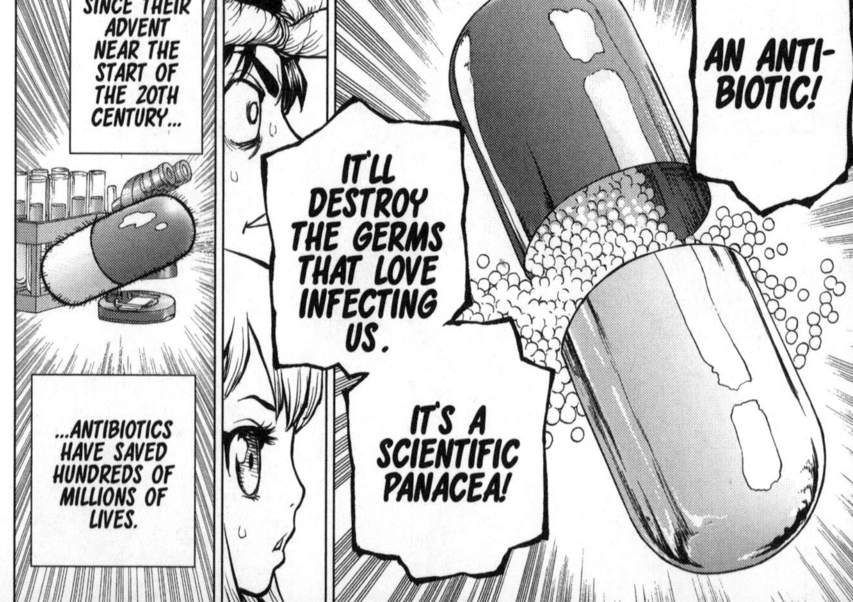
AN ANTI-BIOTIC!
IT'LL DESTROY THE GERMS THAT LOVE INFECTING US.
IT'S A SCIENTIFIC PANACEA!
SINCE THEIR ADVENT NEAR THE START OF THE 20TH CENTURY...
...ANTIBIOTICS HAVE SAVED HUNDREDS OF MILLIONS OF LIVES.

THERE'S NO WAY TO IDENTIFY HER DISEASE WITHOUT RUNNING BLOOD WORK ...
...BUT IT'S STILL WORTH A SHOT!!

OOH, GREAT! LET'S GET STARTED!
WHAT DO WE NEED?!
WE'RE MISSING PRACTICALLY EVERYTHING, SO JUST SIT BACK AND LISTEN.
YOU TWO REMIND ME OF ANOTHER BLOCKHEAD WHO JUMPS BEFORE LOOKING...
Hm?

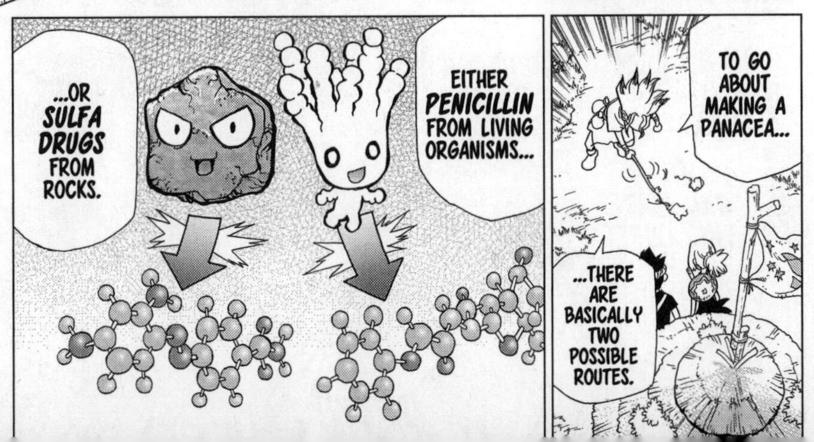
TO GO ABOUT MAKING A PANACEA...
...THERE ARE BASICALLY TWO POSSIBLE ROUTES.
EITHER PENICILLIN FROM LIVING ORGANISMS...
...OR SULFA DRUGS FROM ROCKS.

ORGANSIMS? ROCKS?
HOW DO THEY TURN INTO MEDICINE??
PENICILLIN'S THE MOST WELL-KNOWN. YOU MAKE THAT FROM PENICILLIUM MOLD.
PENICILLIN WAS SO EFFECTIVE IT RELEGATED SULFONAMIDES TO THE ANNALS OF HISTORY.
BUT GOING THE BIOLOGICAL ROUTE, WITH PENICILLIN...
...IN THIS STONE WORLD...
"WHAT A COINCIDENCE! WE JUST HAPPENED TO FIND TEN BILLION PERCENT SUPERPOWERFUL PENICILLIUM LYING AROUND!"
...IS NEVER GONNA HAPPEN. WE'D NEVER GET THAT LUCKY IN THIS GAME OF CHANCE.
BUT IN THE STONE WORLD...
...GOING THE STONE ROUTE, WITH SULFO-NAMIDES...

WE'RE GONNA NEED A TON OF PERSISTENCE AND MANPOWER, BUT...
...THERE'S A TEN BILLION PERCENT CHANCE...
...THAT WE CAN MAKE THIS CURE!

IN THAT CASE...
WHAT'S THE HOLDUP?
YOU STILL DON'T GET IT, CHROME?
I AIN'T A GOD. NOT EVEN A GENIUS, REALLY.
IT ALL HAPPENS STEP BY STEP.
WE GOTTA DO A LOTTA CRAWLING AROUND IN THE DIRT TO GET THERE.

SO...THE STONE ROUTE!!
SKRITCH
SKRITCH
SKRITCH
THIS'LL LEAD TO OUR CURE.
A SCIENTIFIC...
...ROAD MAP!!

START
IRON!
ELEC-
TRICITY!
PHOSPHORUS
COPPER
STRONG
MAGNETS
ALCO-
HOL!
CARBONIC
ACID
VINE-
GAR!
ACETIC
ANHYDRIDE

WHOAAAA
...
FOR
REAL?!
THAT'S
BAAAD!
WE'RE ABOUT TO
WARP THROUGH
TWO MILLION YEARS
OF SCIENTIFIC
PROGRESS.
THERE'S NO
WAY TO DO IT
BUT THROUGH
STEADY
DILIGENCE.

SALT!
HYDRO-CHLORIC ACID
SULFURIC ACID!
CHLOROSULFURIC ACID
SODIUM HYDROXIDE
SODIUM BISULFATE
URINE!
(AMMONIA!)
COAL
SODIUM BI-CARBON-ATE
ANILINE
PANACEA:
SULFO-NAMIDES
GOAL!!
OHHH, SO WE JUST GOTTA START WITH THIS IRON THING!
WHAT'S IRON ANYWAY? TELL ME ALL ABOUT IT.
EVEN THAT WON'T BE EASY.
SO WE'RE GETTING SORCERY... I MEAN, SCIENCE LESSONS FROM SENKU SENSEI?
I FEEL LIKE I'LL NEVER QUITE UNDER-STAND THIS EITHER WAY...

ARE.
YOU.
SERI-OUS?!
BAAAAAD!!
THE EARTH ITSELF IS SPINNING?! BAAAAD!
YESSSSSS. THAT'S RIGHT.
Can't take anymore...
$E=mc^2$

THAT SEEMS ODD.
WHY AREN'T I JUST FLYING OFF OF THIS BRANCH, THEN?
BECAUSE...
...OF GRAVITY.
CROAK CROAK

I ACTUALLY THOUGHT IT WAS WEIRD HOW THAT ONE STAR NEVER MOVES.
THAT REALLY BRIGHT ONE THERE.
THE NORTH STAR.
THERE'S A TEN BILLION PERCENT CHANCE IT POINTS DUE NORTH. REALLY HANDY TO KNOW. TRY TO REMEMBER IT.

WAIT, REALLY?
LOOKS AS THOUGH IT'S SHIFTED A BIT FROM DUE NORTH...
Eyesight: 20/1.8
NOT POSSIBLE.
THE MARGIN OF ERROR IS ONLY...

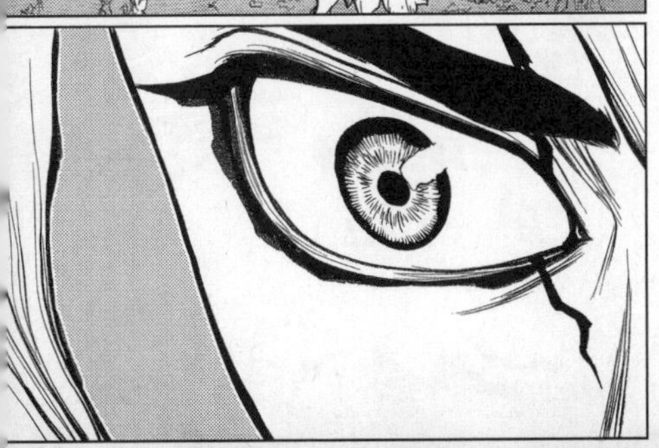

THE EARTH'S AXIS...
...SHIFTED ?!

THE PLANET'S BEEN TILTING LITTLE BY LITTLE OVER THESE PAST 3,700 YEARS.
SO NOW, IN THE YEAR 5739 A.D....
...IT'S DIFFER-ENT!
THE FREAKING NORTH STAR!

NOW I GET HOW MY NAVIGATION WAS OFF ON THE WAY TO HAKONE.
THAT'S HOW I GOT LOST.

HEH HEH HEH... ANY REAL SCIENTIST WOULD BE DISGUSTED AT MY OVERSIGHT...
...BUT YOU GUYS AREN'T HUNG UP ON ANY FIXED NOTIONS...
I'M HOPELESS.

HA! I DON'T THINK...
...YOU'RE HOPELESS AT ALL, SENKU.
NAH, I'M NOT DOWN ON MYSELF.
BUT EVEN I, DESPITE MY COOL HEAD...
...COULDN'T STOP TO CONCEIVE...
...THE SHEER SCALE OF WHAT WE'RE DEALING WITH HERE.
3,700 YEARS!
IT ONLY JUST HIT ME...
...HOW LONG THAT REALLY IS.

...
HM?
HANG ON.
HOW'D YOU GUYS FIGURE OUT THAT THE NORTH STAR DOESN'T POINT DUE NORTH ANYMORE?

OHHHH ?!
SO EVEN THE GREAT SENKU DOESN'T KNOW ABOUT THIS STONE?
MWA HA..A HA HA HA
YES~!
I JUST HAPPENED TO FIND IT OVER ON SOME BARREN HILL.
IT'S ONE BAAAAAD STONE!!

WHEN YOU DANGLE IT OR MAKE IT FLOAT...
...IT ALWAYS POINTS STRAIGHT NORTH.
HOW BAAAD IS THAT?!
BA BAM

A MAGNET...
HE EVEN KNOWS ABOUT THIS? NOOO!!
You call it a magnet?
HEH HEH HEH... GOOD WORK, CHROME!
mc^2
WITH THIS MAGNET...
SPLASH SPLASH SPLASH SPLASH

SPLOOSH
OHHH, LOOK HOW MUCH I FOUND.
LOOKIT ALL THIS CREEPY BLACK SAND!

Iron sand acquired!!
AT LAST, THE VERY FIRST STEP ON OUR ROAD MAP TO THE KINGDOM OF SCIENCE...
START
THE CURTAIN'S RISING ON THE IRON AGE!
GET EXCITED!

Dr.STONE
What's "gravity"?!
The force of attraction between masses...
What's "mass"?!
There's inertial mass and gravitational mass...
What's "inertial"?!
Gahhh! Just google it.
What's "google"?!

Z=21: Dawn of Iron

FINALLY, OUR KINGDOM OF SCIENCE...
THE CURTAIN IS ABOUT TO RISE ON THE IRON AGE!
FSSSHHH
IMPRESSIVE! ARE ALL THE LIONESSES IN YOUR VILLAGE LIKE THIS ONE?
WE HAVE PLENTY OF MONSTROUS GORILLAS, ACTUALLY.
KOHAKU'S THE ONLY NIMBLE GORILLA.
AGAIN, NOT A GORILLA!!

PLUS I'M THE ONLY ONE GETTING ANYTHING DONE HERE!
HOW ABOUT YOU TWO SHOW HOW NIMBLE YOU CAN BE AND GET TO WORK?!
NAHHH...

BOB
BOB
A WATER-MELON...?!
BOB

SPLOSH
WHOA ?!
FWIP
IT'S YOU, SUIKA. WHY ARE YOU HERE?
DID YOU FOLLOW US ALL THIS WAY?
NOD
THE KID'S NAME IS SUIKA??
IT'S JUST A NICKNAME, I THINK.
IT'S BECAUSE OF THAT WATERMELON RIND.
*SUIKA MEANS WATERMELON IN JAPANESE.
SHUP
HEY! WHAT'S THE BIG IDEA, SUIKA?
YOU CAN'T JUST GO STEALING MY MAGNETS!!

!!
IRON SAND!
BUT...
SUIKA JUST WANTS TO HELP.

SUIKA'S ALWAYS WEARING THIS THING...
...SO SUIKA CAN'T REALLY HELP OUT MUCH.
EVEN WHEN SUIKA GROWS UP SOMEDAY.

SO THAT'S WHY IF SOMEONE NEEDS HELP, SUIKA JUST WANTS TO—
GOT IT! YOU MADE YOUR POINT.
!!!

I'M GRATEFUL, TO BE HONEST.
OUR SCIENCE KINGDOM NEEDS ALL THE HELP IT CAN GET. I'M NOT GONNA TURN ANYONE AWAY.
BESIDES, A LITTLE IMP LIKE YOU IS ABOUT TEN BILLION TIMES MORE EFFICIENT AT GATHERING IRON SAND.
HEH HEH HEH... WILL YOU HELP US, SUIKA?
...
SPLASH
SPLASH
FSSH
NO ONE'S EVER...
...NOT ASKED SUIKA...
...WHY SUIKA WEARS THIS THING.
HE MUST'VE REALIZED SUIKA JUST DOESN'T WANNA SHOW SUIKA'S FACE...
...AND DIDN'T BOTHER SUIKA ABOUT IT.
YOU OBVIOUSLY DON'T KNOW SENKU.
THAT'S GIVING HIM TOO MUCH CREDIT.
HE JUST DOESN'T GIVE A CRAP ABOUT YOUR FACE AS LONG AS YOU'RE AN ASSET.

SUISKA'S GONNA GET A TON OF THIS BLACK SAND!
BOB
BOB
ARE YOU MOMOTARO, OR WHAT?!
DON'T DROWN OUT THERE!!
DRAGON QUEST AND MONSTER HUNTER ARE MYSTERIES TO YOU...
IT EVEN MAKES AN APPEARANCE IN DRAGON QUEST.
MONSTER HUNTER?
...BUT YOU KNOW ABOUT MOMOTARO?
WHO TAUGHT YOU THAT?
HEY, YOU KNOW MOMOTARO TOO, SENKU?
RURI TELLS US ALL SORTS OF STORIES!
SPLOOSH

KOHAKU'S THE ONLY NIMBLE GORILLA.
AGAIN, NOT A GORILLA
HEY, GORILLAS TOO. HOW WOULD YOU KNOW ABOUT THEM?
ARE THEY OUT THERE, IN THE WILD?

WE'VE NEVER SEEN ONE IN PERSON.
BUT THERE'S A GORILLA WHO SHOWS UP IN THE TALE OF MOMOTARO.
NO THERE ISN'T!!

IT'S ONE OF THE ANIMAL BUDDIES HE RECRUITS WITH DANGO TREATS, RIGHT?
??

BEAR!
GORILLA!
LION!
CROCODILE...
SINCE WHEN WAS MOMOTARO SO SAVAGE?!
IN THEIR VERSION...
...THE ANIMALS MENTIONED ARE ALL...
...FIERCE AND DANGER-OUS...
I'VE HEARD SO MANY STORIES FROM MY BIG SISTER.
OH, AND RURI ALSO LIKES...
...TO USE BIG, HARD WORDS.

SUDDENLY ...
...MY INTEREST IN THIS RURI HAS BEEN PIQUED.
MAKES ME EVEN MORE DETERMINED TO CURE HER.

?!
YOU'RE INTERESTED IN RURI?
WHAT'S THAT MEAN, SENKU?
HUH?
SENKU... PSST...
SENKU SENSEI...

CHROME
BIG SIS RURI
...
OHHH...
THAT'S HOW IT IS.
I. GOT. IT.

BUT CHROME'S LIKE AN OBLIVIOUS LITTLE KID ABOUT IT.
TOTALLY NOT SELF-AWARE. HAVE TO RESPECT THAT.
?
WHAT?! WHO'RE YOU CALLING A KID?!

That golden spear is niiiice.
GLINT
I JUST WANNA HAVE A LITTLE CHAT WITH RURI, OKAY?
LIKE I SAID, YOU WON'T BE TAKING ONE STEP INTO THE VILLAGE!
RULES ARE RULES!!
WELL, ONCE WE COOK UP A CURE, THEY'LL HAVE NO CHOICE...
...BUT TO LET US IN.
SO LET'S GET STARTED!

THE DAWN OF THE SCIENCE KINGDOM...
...STARTS WITH IRON!!

SO THIS BLACK SAND FROM THE RIVER...
...IS GONNA TURN INTO IRON?
YEP. JUST GOTTA COMBINE FOUR PARTS IRON SAND WITH ONE PART CHARCOAL AND MELT IT ALL DOWN.
4
1
OOH... HOW SIMPLE!
HEH HEH HEH... DON'T GET EXCITED JUST YET.
THIS AIN'T ANYTHING LIKE BAKING POTTERY.

WOOD BURNS AT A NICE AND TOASTY...
...700 DEGREES, AT BEST.
BUT TURNING IRON SAND INTO IRON...
...THAT SORTA PROCESS REQUIRES...
...1,500 DEGREES!

CAN WE GET IT HOT ENOUGH?
HOW DO WE DO IT?
GOTTA BLOW REAL HARD!
WE HAVE NO CHOICE BUT TO FEED THE FIRE HEAPS OF OXYGEN.
BLOWING ALL THAT AIR IN THERE WITHOUT PAUSE...
...IS LIKE CASTING A "POWER BOOST" SPELL THAT'LL BOOST THE TEMP FROM 700 TO 1,500 DEGREES!!

TOSS
TOSS
TOSS

LITTLE GUSTS OF WIND! WITH SOMETHING AS HANDY AS THIS...
...I COULD PROBABLY DO THE JOB MYSELF!
YOU'LL REGRET THOSE WORDS.
YOU CAN'T HAVE TOO MANY PEOPLE FOR THIS.

FWOOOM
FWOOSH
FWOOSH
FWOOSH
FWOOSH
FWOOSH
FWOOSH
FWOOSH
FWOOSH
FWOOSH

FWOOOM
FWOOSH
FWOOSH FWOOSH
FWOOSH
FWOOSH
FWOOSH
FWOOSH

GAHHHH MY ARMS'RE ABOUT TO FALL OFF!
DON'T STOP OR THE TEMPERATURE'LL DROP!
FWOOSH FWOOSH
HOW MANY MORE MINUTES OF THIS?
FWOOSH FWOOSH
FWOOSH
FWOOSH
FWOOSH

RIGHT. APPROXI-MATELY...

...A FEW DOZEN HOURS!
MANU-FACTURING IRON IS BAAAAAD !!!
LIMP
LIMP
SAVE YOURSELF, SUIKA.
TAKE A REST!

*Note: *Gin* means silver and *kin* means gold in Japanese.

CHIRP
CHIRP

WHAK

FSSHH
...
RECRUITING LABOR...
...IS THE TOP PRIORITY!
I GUESS WE NEED MORE CITIZENS FOR OUR SCIENCE KINGDOM.

SPEAR ...
A SILVER ONE...
HEH HEH HEH... GINRO'S BASICALLY ALREADY WON OVER.
LET'S JUST KEEP UP THE PATTERN.
USING SCIENCEY BAIT TO CONVINCE THEM!!
Z Z Z
BUT SHINY SPEARS AIN'T GONNA WORK ON EACH AND EVERY VILLAGER.
WE NEED SOME INTEL.
GOTTA FIND OUT WHAT EACH OF THEM CRAVES.
SUIKA IS REALLY GOOD AT THAT SORTA THING.
SUIKA CAN JUST BE DISGUISED AS A WATER-MELON...
...AND SNEAK AROUND LEARNING THINGS.
SWIP SWIP
PLUNK
OHHHH!
HEH HEH HEH... NOT BAD!
AWESOME! IN THE CONTINUED QUEST FOR IRON-WORKERS...
...GREAT DETECTIVE SUIKA IS ON THE CASE!!

Dr. STONE
Big Sis Ruri's
SAVAGE MOMOTARO
Why, something's poking out.
BOB
Something awfully muscular...
BOB

E=mc²
Z=22: Survival Gourmet

WE CAN MAKE IRON!!
WE JUST NEED TO FIRST RECRUIT MORE ALLIES!!

TO GET MORE LABOR...
...ALL WE NEED IS SOME SCIENCEY BAIT!!
SCIENCE
MWAHAHAHA
STOP CALLING IT BAIT, YOU TWO.
FIRST WE NEED INTEL ON WHO CAN BE LURED OVER TO OUR SIDE.
WE'RE COUNTING ON YOU FOR THAT, GREAT DETECTIVE SUIKA!!

GREAT DETECTIVE ...
...SUIKA!!
TAH DAH

SWIP
SWIP

POP!

ROLL ROLL ROLL

CHATTER
CHATTER

BADUM
BADUM
SO WHAT HAPPENED WITH THAT OUTSIDER KOHAKU BROUGHT IN?
THE CHIEF SAYS THERE'S NO NEED TO PROVOKE HIM IF HE ISN'T FORCING HIS WAY INTO THE VILLAGE.
AND I AGREE.
GET THIS, GET THIS... I HEAR HE'S CAMPING OUT AT CHROME'S PLACE!
BUT IF THE GUY STARTS STIRRING UP TROUBLE...

KRAKL
KRAKL
SO SUIKA WENT AROUND ALL DAY...
...FINDING OUT WHAT PEOPLE WANT!!

FIRST UP...
GARNET, SAPPHIRE AND RUBY—THE THREE SPARKLY SISTERS.
OOH, THE PRETTIEST GIRLS IN THE VILLAGE.
WHAT THEY WANT MORE THAN ANYTHING IS...
BETTER BE SOMETHING WE CAN MAKE WITH STONE WORLD SCIENCE.

BAM
BOYFRIENDS!
What's a boyfriend anyway?
NO CHANCE OF MAKING ONE OF THOSE WITH SCIENCE!!

A STRONG MAN.
A HOTTIE.
A GOOD PROVIDER.
AT LEAST THEY'RE HONEST ABOUT THEIR DESIRES...
BLAB BLAB

HAH! YOU SEEM TO BE QUITE THE LADIES' MAN, SENKU...
...BUT UNFORTUNATELY I DON'T THINK YOU'RE WHAT SAPPHIRE MEANS BY HOTTIE.

WHATEVER. GIRLS'RE ALWAYS RUNNING THEIR MOUTHS LIKE THAT.
THAT'S WHY I DON'T LIKE 'EM, Y'KNOW.
WHAT A CHILD YOU ARE, CHROME! RURI AND I ARE GIRLS. DO YOU HATE US TOO?
I DON'T SEE YOU AS A GIRL, KOHAKU. MORE LIKE A GORILLA.

Sorry.

THE ONE WHO WANTS A PROVIDER COULD BE OUR ONLY SHOT.
WHAT'S SHE AFTER, REALLY?
E=mc²
TASTY FISH TO EAT.

AH!
SPEAKING OF FOOD...
THERE'S ALSO THE VILLAGE GLUTTON, GANEN.
HE COMPLAINS EVERY DAY ABOUT HOW HE'S SO SICK OF FISH HE COULD DIE!
HE'S ALWAYS LOOKING FOR NEW SORTS OF FOOD.

KRAKL
KRAKL
KRAKL
I KNOW JUST THE RIGHT SCIENTIFIC BAIT...
...TO GET US SOME ALLIES!!
HEH HEH HEH... GREAT DETECTIVE SUIKA, INDEED!
THINGS'RE FALLING INTO PLACE.

WE'RE REALLY JUST COOKING SOMETHING?
THAT'S GOT NOTHING TO DO WITH SCIENCE.
NOTHING TO DO WITH IT?
FOOD IS SCIENCE, BUD.
WHAT DO YOU THINK GIVES THAT UMAMI FLAVOR TO THE FISH YOU PEOPLE EAT EVERY DAY?
GLUTAMIC ACID AND INOSINIC ACID.

WHIP WHIP

SUIKA. WHAT'S THAT YOU GOT THERE?
THIS THING?
WELL, SUIKA'S FRIEND, CHALK...
THIS IS HIS FAVORITE TOY.

SUIKA CALLS IT A DOGTAIL.
THAT'S FOXTAIL GRASS, ACTUALLY.
TWITCH
TMP
BAM
WITH ENOUGH FOXTAILS LIKE THAT ONE...
...I MIGHT JUST BE ABLE TO MAKE IT!
IT'S A DISH BELOVED BY EVERYONE IN THE PREVIOUS WORLD.
THE WORLD'S...
...MOST DELICIOUS MEAL!

STARTING FROM SCRATCH.
IT'S TIME FOR SOME PRIMAL SURVIVAL GOURMET.
GET EXCITED!!

WOOF WOOF!
WOOF WOOF WOOF!
THWUMP

SMAK
SMAK
SMAK

YOU'RE SAYING WE CAN REALLY EAT THESE FOXTAILS?
HAH! I THINK I'LL PASS.
NOT LIKE THIS... BUT BEATING THEM STARTS THE THRESHING PROCESS.

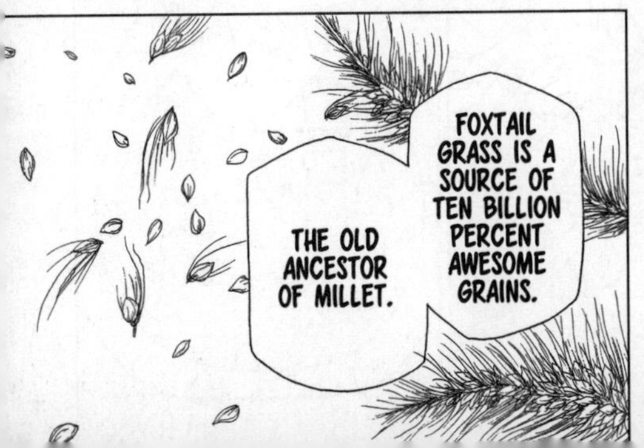
FOXTAIL GRASS IS A SOURCE OF TEN BILLION PERCENT AWESOME GRAINS.
THE OLD ANCESTOR OF MILLET.

HM... JUST LOOKS SORT OF DIRTY TO ME.
LOOKIT ALL THOSE HAIR-LOOKING THINGS!
SHOMP

JUST NEED A PLAN...
...AND PLENTY OF TRIAL AND ERROR.
FIBERS
CHAFF
GRAINS

BECAUSE FOOD...
...IS STILL JUST SCIENCE!

KRST KRST
KRST KRST
IT MIGHT NOT BE WHEAT FLOUR, BUT THIS FOXTAIL FLOUR...
...IS READY!!

KRAK
MIX SOME WILD BIRD EGGS INTO OUR FLOUR.
A LITTLE LYE FROM ASH.
POTASSIUM CARBONATE FOR ELASTICITY.
SOME NAMELESS MONGOL IN THE FOURTH CENTURY STUMBLED UPON THIS RECIPE...
THIS DISH OF SCIENCE...
SOMEONE JUST LIKE YOU, CHROME.
HE WAS SOME BAAAD DUDE RUNNING AROUND, TRYING EVERYTHING...
...IN FOURTH CENTURY MONGOLIA.
TOK TOK

GURGL
GURGL
GURGL

TH—
TH- THAT AROMA!
WAY BACK...
3,700 YEARS AGO...
WE ENJOYED THIS DELICIOUS DISH OF SCIENCE!

WE CALL THIS...
...RAMEN!

HEH HEH HEH... KEEP IN MIND, THIS PRIMEVAL GOURMET MEAL...
...IS PROBABLY ABOUT TEN BILLION TIMES WORSE THAN THE STUFF PRODUCED BY THOSE CLASSY, DEDICATED CHEFS.
BUT ALL THAT'S REALLY BEHIND IT...
...IS THOSE FOXTAILS?
I'M OUR OFFICIAL TASTE TESTER.
DIVING RIGHT INTO NEW AND MYSTERIOUS THINGS WITHOUT HESITATION...
...IS JUST THE SORCERER'S WAY OF LIFE!
SLURP

YUMMMMM!!
SLURP
RAMEN IS BAAAAD!!
SLURP
WAHHH, IT'S SO SLURPY! LIKE, HOW YOU EAT IT.
SUIKA'S NEVER HAD ANYTHING LIKE IT!!
HARD TO BELIEVE FOOD SO INCREDIBLE COULD EXIST IN THIS WORLD...

HEH HEH HEH... GUESS I'D BETTER HAVE A TASTE.
THE FIRST DECENT GOURMET CUISINE...
...IN 3,700 YEARS.
WELL, DECENT MIGHT BE GOING TOO FAR.

NOT DECENT...
...AT ALL.
BECAUSE I WAS FORCED TO USE FOXTAILS... SO BLAND AND TASTELESS.
AND THAT NASTY, BITTER AFTERTASTE...
Just gotta think of it as herbal, medicinal cooking??

BUT TO THOSE GUYS...
...IT'S A GIFT FROM THE GODS.
THIS IS GONNA WORK.
FOXTAIL RAMEN!!

BWOOP BWOOP
BWOOP BWOOP BWOOP BWOOP ♫
JUST LIKE HOW WARS HAVE BEEN STARTED OVER PEPPER...
...FOOD HAS ALWAYS BEEN AT THE ROOT OF CIVILIZATION!

WITH THE POWER OF RAMEN...
...THIS VILLAGE WILL BE MINE TO COMMAND!!
FROM YOUR ACTIONS, IT JUST SEEMS LIKE YOU'RE A NICE GUY SHARING THIS TASTY FOOD WITH EVERYONE.
BUT EVERY WORD OUT OF YOUR MOUTH SOUNDS DOWNRIGHT EVIL.
WHAT'S THE MEANING OF THIS?!
SOME-THING...
...SMELLS REAL TASTY!!
BWOOP BWOOP

Who's the most popular hunk or babe among the villagers?

Karin from Kanagawa Prefecture SEARCH

1st Place: Magma

2nd Place: Kinro

3rd Place: Argo

4th Place: Carbo

5th Place: Ginro

Science Questions	How does one make gasoline out of plastic bottle caps?
Character Questions	If Taiju and Tsukasa really fought, who would win?
Questions That Aren't Really Questions	I wanna get petrified and challenge myself to count the seconds...

Dr.STONE

Z=23: The Smooth Talker
$E=mc^2$

CHATTER
CHATTER
LADY KOHAKU... I MEAN, KOHAKU...
...SEEMS TO BE HANDING OUT FOOD TO THE VILLAGERS.
SHALL WE GO, CHIEF?
GO WHERE?
TO EAT, I MEAN.
NOT A CHANCE.
BAM
KOHAKU.
JUST WHAT ARE YOU UP TO...
...WITH THAT OUTSIDER YOU BROUGHT?

BWOOP
BWOOP
SCIENCE GOURMET!
I CAN USE THIS FOXTAIL RAMEN...
...TO RECRUIT CITIZENS...
...FOR MY IRON-MAKING KINGDOM OF SCIENCE!!
BAM
GULP

SLURRP
SO SPRINGY AND AMAZING!
JUST... INCREDIBLE!
RAMEN
BA-DUM BA-DUM
HEH HEH. WE ALL KNOW YOU LIVE TO EAT, GANEN, SO IF THAT'S YOUR VERDICT...
HERE I GO!

YOU'RE THE MAN WHO WHIPPED UP THIS DELICIOUS MEAL? ♡
SENKU, WAS IT?
WHEN IT COMES TO GIRLS, WHAT'S YOUR TYPE?
GIRLS WHO CAN PUMP TONS OF OXYGEN INTO AN IRON FORGE.
YOU REALLY HAVE NO CLUE HOW TO BE SUBTLE, DO YOU, SENKU?
YOU'RE TOO BLUNT!!
HEY, KINRO, GINRO. YOU GUYS SHOULD HAVE SOME TOO!
THIS RAMEN STUFF IS BAAAAD, I'M TELLING YA!
KEKEKE
WE WOULD NEVER CONSUME YOUR DUBIOUS SORCERER'S FARE!
SHP
SENTRIES HAVE NO BUSINESS ACCEPTING FOOD IN THE FIRST PLACE.
RULES ARE RULES!
OH? THEN WHY DO YOU STILL HAVE THAT SPEAR?
FOOD IS UNACCEPTABLE, BUT TREASURES ARE JUST FINE?
SHE'S GOT YOU THERE.
TWINGE
TWINGE

HEY, THE NOODLES'RE GETTING ALL MUSHY WHILE YOU WASTE TIME ARGUING!
HOW MANY BOWLS HAVE YOU HAD?
MAKES A MAN THIRSTY. WHAT I WOULDN'T GIVE FOR A COLA RIGHT NOW.
COLA??

A FRIEND OF YOURS, SENKU?
NO.
THAT'S ENOUGH SQUABBLING, KINRO, GINRO.
WHAT? WHY...?
IN SHORT, WE HAVE...

AN ENEMY.
FWOOSH

SHINK
SHINK
SHINK
SHINK
SHINK

EXPLAIN YOURSELF. UNLESS YOU WANT YOUR THROAT SLICED OPEN!
DO YOU SERVE THE LONG-HAIRED MAN?!
IT'S EASY TO FEEL STRONG AND COOL...
...WHEN FIGHTING BY KOHAKU'S SIDE.
OH DEAR. NOT THAT I DON'T LIKE GETTING INTERROGATED BY SUCH A CUTIE, BUT...
...I'M AFRAID YOU'VE MISTAKEN ME FOR SOMEONE ELSE.

I DON'T KNOW ANY LONG-HAIRED MAN.
EVER SINCE BREAKING OUT OF THE STONE...
...I'VE BEEN ALL BY MY LONESOME...

!
I THOUGHT I RECOGNIZED THAT FACE.
YOU'RE GEN ASAGIRI!
MAGIC
CHOLOGY
BY GEN ASAGIRI
SO YOU KNOW HIM?!
NOPE. NOT EVEN ONE MILLI-METER.
HE'S JUST SOME MAGICIAN WHO WROTE A TRASHY BOOK ON PSYCHOLOGY.
YOU'VE READ MY WORK? HOW WONDERFUL. CALLING IT TRASHY IS A BIT CRUEL, THOUGH.
AND PLEASE, CALL ME A *MENTALIST.*

I SUPPOSE I SHOULD APOLOGIZE FOR SNEAKING A BOWL OF RAMEN.
SO WHY DON'T YOU ALL JUST LOWER YOUR WEAPONS?
I'M SO SCARED MY HANDS ARE SHAKING.
WOULDN'T WANT TO SPILL EVEN A DROP OF THIS PRECIOUS RAMEN.
I-I-I'LL TAKE IT OFF YOUR HANDS.

...
EVERY SINGLE THING HE SAYS IS A LIE.
HE'S NOT AFRAID AT ALL.

THERE I WAS, SEARCHING FOR TODAY'S MEAL, SO IMAGINE MY SURPRISE!
THAT NOSTALGIC AROMA OF RAMEN NEARLY HAD ME REELING.
IT'S LIKE EVERY WORD OUT OF HIS MOUTH HAS WINGS...
SO LIGHT AND AIRY...!!

...

HEH HEH HEH... I GUESS I'LL BUY YOUR STORY.
BUT THERE'S NO FREE LUNCH IN THIS WORLD, Y'KNOW?
PLENTY OF WORK TO BE DONE BY EVERYONE WHO'S ENJOYED THIS RAMEN!
WORK?
LIKE WASHING DISHES?

RAHHHHHH!
FWOOM

THIS IS THE MODDED, SOUPED-UP VERSION OF THE BELLOWS SYSTEM.
IRON FORGE LEVEL 2!
DWSH
DWSH

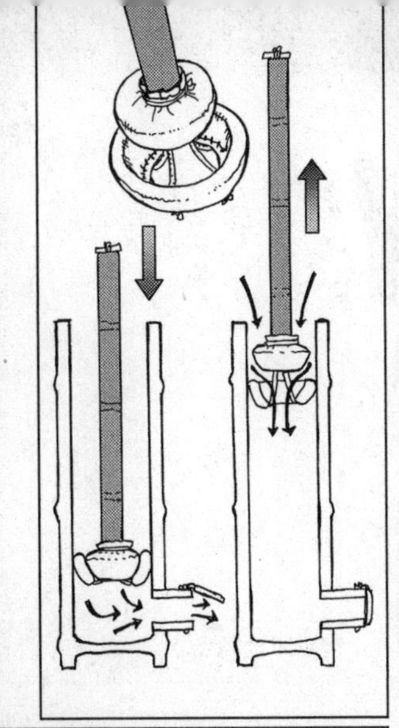

THIS NEW SHIFTING METHOD REALLY WORKS...!!

GEN ASAGIRI.
$E=mc^2$
HOW'RE TAIJU AND YUZURIHA DOING THESE DAYS?

AH, SO THAT'S YOUR GAME?
PULL ONE OVER ON ME WHILE I'M DISTRACTED AND SLAVING AWAY?
PWOOSH
PWOOSH
YOU'RE A BRAVE MAN.
TO CHALLENGE A MENTALIST TO THAT SORT OF BATTLE.
BUT DON'T WORRY.

THEY'RE DOING JUST FINE.
ESPECIALLY TAIJU, WITH HIS BOTTOMLESS STAMINA!
BUT YOU KNOW ALL ABOUT THAT...
...SENKU.

!
SO HE IS WORKING FOR LONG-HAIR!
SHOULD I KILL HIM?!
WAIT, YOU FOOL.
GEN ASAGIRI...
YOU WERE TEN BILLION PERCENT ONTO US FROM THE START.
SO WHY JUST LET IT SLIP SO EASILY THAT YOU'RE TSUKASA'S PAL?
BECAUSE THE DYNAMIC CHANGED...
...WHEN I SAW ALL THIS.
FWOOOM

FSSHH

IN ALL HONESTY ...
THERE WAS NO DOUBT IN MY MIND THAT TSUKASA'S EMPIRE WOULD WIN.
CLEARLY.

MY JOB WAS TO CONFIRM YOUR DEATH ONCE AND FOR ALL, SENKU.
SO IF I WENT BACK AND SAID, "TSUKASA! SENKU'S STILL ALIVE!" WELL, YOU'D MEET YOUR END SOON ENOUGH.
THAT WAS THE PLAN.

BUT NOW THAT IRON WEAPONS ARE IN PLAY...
WHO CAN SAY HOW THE TIDES OF WAR MAY SHIFT?!

SO I'LL JUST FEED HIM SOME LIES.
"ALL I DISCOVERED WAS A PRIMITIVE SETTLEMENT." "SENKU IS GOOD AND DEAD."
IN EFFECT, I'LL BE SAVING YOU.
HEH HEH HEH... I'D REALLY APPRECIATE THAT.

I DON'T HOLD ANY HARD-AND-FAST POLICIES.
I'M JUST THE WORLD'S SMOOTHEST TALKER.
LIVING A LIFE OF EASE WITH A HORDE OF CUTE GIRLS IS ALL I WANT.
IT DOESN'T MATTER TO ME WHETHER IT'S YOU OR TSUKASA WHO ENDS UP DEAD.

BUT I'M AT A LOSS NOW. SHOULD I BETRAY TSUKASA AND JOIN YOU, SENKU?!
IT'S THE TSUKASA EMPIRE VERSUS YOUR KINGDOM OF SCIENCE.
WHICH WILL TRIUMPH, IN THE END?
FLAP
E=mc²
I ALWAYS BET ON THE WINNING HORSE...
...NO MATTER WHOM I HAVE TO CUT LOOSE!

HUH? AIN'T IT OBVIOUS ALREADY?
THE KINGDOM OF SCIENCE.
GLINT
AHHHH!
FINALLY ...!!
Iron acquired!!

Gen Asagiri's

Magic Psychology

Let's have a look inside!

Question: You're going on a school trip and hoping to make friends with a classmate you've never spoken to before. You're thrilled to have this chance, but whom do you choose?

1. President of the Science Club
2. A reliable tough guy
3. A strong tomboy
4. An outdoorsy adventurer

Results Analysis:

Whomever you chose represents what you feel is missing most in your life. If you're hoping to break out of that rut, go out and buy whichever item matches your result!

1. A new computer
2. A jogging outfit
3. Expensive, fancy clothes
4. A barbecue grill

I SLAPPED THIS BOOK TOGETHER WITHOUT MUCH THOUGHT...

Z=24: Lightning Speed!!

BUZZ
BUZZ
SO IT'S SENKU VERSUS TSUKASA.
WHOSE VICTORY WOULD I ENJOY MORE?
THAT'S ALL I'M INTERESTED IN KNOWING.
TREASURES CREATED BY SCIENCE!
LIKE RAMEN!
BUT BACK-BREAKING WORK!!
IF WE REVIVE SOME IDOLS...
I GET MY DREAM HAREM!!
EASY LIVING!!
THE REST OF YOU, BE HONEST...
WHICH WOULD YOU PREFER?

WHAT'S A "HAIR-M"?
AH, SORRY. IT'S NOTHING A CHILD LIKE YOU NEEDS TO KNOW ABOUT.
SUIKA JUST WANTS MORE OF THIS RAMEN STUFF!
RAMEN IS NICE, YES, BUT A LITTLE HOT.
PUFF
PUFF
COOL COOL
TILT
I'M LEANING TOWARD TEAM TSUKASA AT THIS POINT.
BUZZ
BUZZ
GEN ASAGIRI, RIGHT? A SHALLOW, SELF-SERVING MAN LIKE YOU...
...NEEDS TO BE KILLED OR LOCKED UP.
KSHNK
YIKES! SCARY!
IF WE DON'T SEND HIM HOME TO TSUKASA, THAT IDIOT'S GONNA BE KNOCKING DOWN OUR DOOR BEFORE WE KNOW IT. THAT'D BE CHECK-MATE!
What happened to Gen?
Is Senku alive after all?

HEH HEH HEH... REST EASY, BUD.
WE'RE GONNA USE OUR AWESOME NEW IRON TO CREATE SOMETHING ELSE.
WHEN YOU SEE IT, YOU'LL BE TEN BILLION PERCENT BEHIND TEAM SCIENCE.
OHH? WHAT COULD IT BE?
A KATANA OR SOMETHING?

A POWER PLANT!

ERIOUSLY-SAY...? ARE YOU PULLING MY LEG??
NO. THAT'D BE AS HARD AS SOME CRAZY-HARD VIDEO GAME!!
DON'TCHA HAVE ANY NATIVE COPPER AROUND HERE?
C'MON, THAT STUFF'S TOO PRETTY TO DESTROY!
I'M GONNA MELT IT DOWN TO MAKE WIRE.
NO WAY!
THEN...
WE JUST NEED SOME LIGHTNING.
FWASH
RMBBBB

WE'RE ABOUT TO GET SOME...!
RRMBB
HAH! IT IS STORM SEASON, AFTER ALL.
RRMBB
TOO LUCKY, MAN!!
LUCKY? NOT AT ALL, FOOLS. THIS IS TERRIBLE.
I'M NOT EVEN ONE MILLIMETER PREPARED FOR THIS!!

WAH!
GAH!

RRMMBB
LIGHTNING IS COMING! IT'S HEAVEN'S RAGE!
GET STRUCK AND YOU'RE DEAD!
WOMEN AND CHILDREN, FIND COVER!!

SO THIS LIGHTNING WILL POWER YOUR PLANT?
OF COURSE NOT.
DIDN'T THINK SO.
BUT WITH A GOOD MAGNET...
...I CAN CREATE A DYNAMO.
MAGNET? HOW ABOUT THE ONES WE COLLECTED IRON SAND WITH?
NATURAL MAGNETS LIKE THAT WON'T COME CLOSE TO CUTTING IT.
TOMP
IF LIGHTNING STRIKES OUR IRON ROD...
CHATTER
...WE CAN MAKE A HIGH-STRENGTH MAGNET...
...WITH THE POWER OF SCIENCE!!
I WAS GONNA PUT UP A LIGHTNING ROD AND SIT AROUND WAITING LIKE AN IDIOT...
...SO WE CAN'T LET THIS CHANCE GO TO WASTE. GOTTA SET IT UP REALLY FAST!!
WE GOTTA GO AT...

LIGHT-
NING...
...SPEED!!
FIRST, MELT DOWN THAT COPPER!
FWOOM
THAT'S LACQUER ON YOUR SHIELD, RIGHT, KOHAKU?
WHERE DO YOU KEEP LACQUER IN THIS VILLAGE?
SWIPSWIPSWIP
SUIKA'S GOT THE LACQUER!!

LACQUER MAKES FOR A GRADE-A INSULATOR.
GO AHEAD AND COAT THE IRON WITH IT.
GLOOP
WHAT ...??
GAH! WHAT'RE YOU DOING WITH THAT BRIDGE PLANK?!
SNAP
I JUST HAVE TO CARVE...
...ONE LONG GROOVE INTO THIS BOARD, RIGHT?!
SKLIT
POUR THE MELTED COPPER INTO THE GROOVE.
SHZZ
TAKE THE HARDENED WIRE...
...AND WRAP IT ALL AROUND THE IRON ROD!!
TWIST TWIST

OH NO OH NO OH NO! THE OUTSIDER AND HIS FRIENDS'RE DESTROYING THE BRIDGE!
MWA HA HA! SO HE'S FINALLY REVEALED HIS WICKED NATURE?!

HEY, Y'THINK THEY WENT AND CALLED THIS WITH THEIR SORCERY?
THIS HEAVEN'S RAGE?!
I'LL KILL 'EM ALL. LEAVE IT TO ME!!
OKAAAY ...

TOMP
TOMP
!!

TOMP
TOMP

BAAAD NEWS!
IT'S MAGMA!
HE'S NOT A MAN TO BE REASONED WITH.
WE CAN'T AVOID A FIGHT!
ALL-OUT WAR AGAINST THE VILLAGE AT THIS POINT MEANS GAME OVER.
CRAP! WE NEED A WAY OUTTA THIS...

HM...
THIS WON'T DO.
I'D RATHER NOT BE KILLED SIMPLY FOR FRATERNIZING WITH YOU.

FIND ME SOME FLOWERS, WOULD YOU, SUIKA?
FLOWERS...
...TRUMP WAR!
TMP

BE-
AM...

HUH? THIS SMUG JERK CAME TO BRING US FLOWERS?
YOU THE ONE WHO CALLED DOWN HEAVEN'S RAGE?
MWA HA HA! MIGHTY BRAVE OF YOU, STEPPING FORWARD TO DIE.

NOOO, JUST THE OPPOSITE.
YOU SEE, WE'RE ACTUALLY...
...USING SORCERY ...
...TO MAKE THAT MEAN OLD LIGHTNING VANISH.
YEAH? SOUNDS LIKE A BUNCH OF CRAP TO ME...
JUST LIKE SO.

BAM
?!!
THEY REALLY VANISHED!
RIGHT BEFORE OUR EYES!
IMPOSSIBLE ...
HE'S SIMPLY HIDDEN THEM...
...FROM MAGMA'S GANG!
BACK-PALMING TECHNIQUE, HUH?
FWIP
HEH HEH HEH... NOT BAD, YOU QUACK MAGICIAN!

RRMMBBB
FSSHHH
A CRAZY-HARD VIDEO GAME? HARDLY.
AT NASA, OLD MAN VASILEVSKIY...
...CONDUCTED SUCCESSFUL EXPERIMENTS CREATING MAGNETS IN PLACES WITH LOTS OF LIGHTNING.
New Mexico NASA
I JUST HAPPENED TO FIND IT OVER ON SOME BARREN HILL!!
IT'S ONE BAAAAD STONE!!
CHROME...
THESE ARE THE FRUITS OF YOUR DECADE-LONG BATTLE!
OH YEAH? YOU IMPRESSED YET?

KRRRACK
HERE WE ARE! THE BARREN HILL!
THE PERFECT SPOT FOR LIGHT-NING!
IF IT'S GONNA STRIKE, IT'LL BE HERE!
KRRRACK
KRRRACK
SO THEY'RE BUILDING A TOWER?
SHOULD WE HELP...?
YOU'RE JUST AFTER A SILVER SPEAR, AREN'T YOU, GINRO?!
OUR JOB IS TO STAND GUARD.
RULES ARE RULES!
THE LIGHTNING'S CLOSE!
CRAP! BY THE TIME WE SET UP THIS SCAFFOLDING FOR THE LIGHTNING ROD...
IT'LL BE TOO LATE!

FSHHH
TCH... IF ONLY WE HAD SOMETHING LONG...
...TO STICK INTO THE GROUND...

N...
NO!
ANYTHING BUT MY SPEAR!
SEE. I KNEW YOU LIKED IT.

WHAP
SHWIP
TUG
THUNK
...

HEH HEH HEH... HERE IT COMES.
THE GOD OF ELEC-TRICITY!
MY SPEEEEAR!
KRAACK
THAT SPEAR'S ABOUT TO GET US OUR DYNAMO...
IN THE FORM OF A POWERFUL MAGNET!!

KRRR
GENERATING POWER?
IN THIS STONE WORLD??
FOR...
...REAL...?!
KERBAM

SENKU

Z=25: By These Hands, the Light of Science

KRRR RRAK

HA HA HA HA! THIS IS INSANE, SENKU.
IN THIS BARREN STONE WORLD, STARTING WITH NOTHING...
...YOU'VE REALLY DONE IT...

ELEC-TRICITY IS IN PLAY!
GET EXCITED!!

CHF
RIBBIT

SO THE GOLD SPEAR'S JUST DUST IN THE WIND!
YOU'LL HAVE TO FORGIVE ME, KINRO.
IT WAS AN EMERGENCY.
SUIKA BETS THAT SENKU'LL MAKE YOU ANOTHER ONE!

WHAT COULD HAVE HAPPENED TO THAT GOLD SPEAR? GONE FOREVER, IS IT?!
THE SPEAR ONLY YOU GOT!
THE GOLD SPEAR THAT YOU WOULDN'T EVEN LET ME BORROW!!
FSSHH

!!
SENKU, I FEAR...
...OUR ATTEMPT TO MAKE MAGNETS HAS FAILED!
?!!

INSTEAD OF COMING TOGETHER...
...SOME MYSTERIOUS FORCE IS PUSHING THEM APART!!
WIGGLE
WIGGLE
THE POLES ARE SWITCHED.

SWIP
KASHUNG
OHHHHH!
WHOA, THAT'S STRONG!
Strong magnets acquired!

START
IRON
STRONG MAGNETS
ELEC-TRICITY
WE CAN MAKE IT NOW, RIGHT?
THAT BAAAD THING YOU CALLED ELECTRICITY!!
BUT, SENKU, WILL THE ELECTRICITY COME FROM...
THERMAL POWER?
WIND POWER?
DON'T TELL ME... NUCLEAR POWER?

MANPOWER!
RIGHT. SHOULD'VE KNOWN.

KLANG
KLANG
HAMMER THAT SHEET OF COPPER AND STRETCH IT OUT...
CUT AWAY THE EXCESS...
...TO FORM A DISK!
GET A LOAD OF THIS! IT'S THAT BAAAD, SUPER-HARD ROCK I SHOWED YOU.
THIS CORUNDUM CAN GRIND IT DOWN!!
THAT'S THE NEXT-HARDEST ROCK, AFTER DIAMOND.
THE CHROME COLLECTION STRIKES GOLD AGAIN.

WHY'S YOUR FACE ALL PUFFED UP LIKE A MARSH-MALLOW?
LACQUER POISONING.
UM, SENKU. I'VE BEEN RACKING MY BRAIN...
...TRYING TO COME UP WITH JUST THE RIGHT QUIP.
I WAS THINKING WE'D USE PHOSPHORIC ACID TO COAT THE COPPER WIRE, BUT...
...THIS LACQUER WORKS JUST FINE!
KLANG
KLANG
KLANG
KLANG
NICE!
HEH HEH HEH... THE SCIENCE KINGDOM'S SPECIAL-MADE...
BAM
...DUAL HAND-CRANKED DYNAMO...
...IS COMPLETE!!
SENKU
SENKU
Dynamo acquired!!

S
N
SO BOTH DISKS HAVE TO BE TURNED AT ONCE!
SEEMS HARD.
IT JUST NEEDS TWO PEOPLE TO DO IT!
THE WHOLE THING'LL FALL TO PIECES IF THEY DON'T SYNC UP.
YEP.
BUT WHERE'RE WE GONNA FIND A PHYSICALLY CAPABLE PAIR WHO CAN MOVE IN PERFECT UNISON?
FWOOSH

ELECTRICITY SURE IS WONDERFUL, SENKU!
IN A SCIENTIFIC CIVILIZA-TION...
IN OUR WORLD OF SORCERY...
TV
...EVERY WONDERFUL DEVICE AND CONTRAPTION WAS POWERED BY ELECTRICITY.
WITH A BIT OF ELEC-TRICITY...
SMOOTH
SMOOTH
GOLD AND SILVER SPEARS...
...WOULD BE POSSIBLE. WE COULD EVEN REPAIR THEM...
...RIGHT, SENKU?!

GILDING THINGS VIA ELECTRICITY IS TOUGH. DO YOU EVEN KNOW HOW TO DO THAT?
NOT A CLUE.
I SWEAR, GEN ASAGIRI.
EVERY WORD OUT OF YOUR MOUTH IS AS FLEETING AS A BIRD ON THE WING...

GAHHHHH!
SNIPSNIPSNIPSNIPSNIP

SPEAR ARMY
RAMEN ARMY
WE'RE BUILDING UP A DECENT LINEUP OF CITIZENS FOR THE KINGDOM OF SCIENCE!!
HEH HEH HEH... KINRO AND GINRO ARE MINE NOW.
RAHHHH
OF COURSE THOSE BROTHERS WOULD BE IN SYNC.

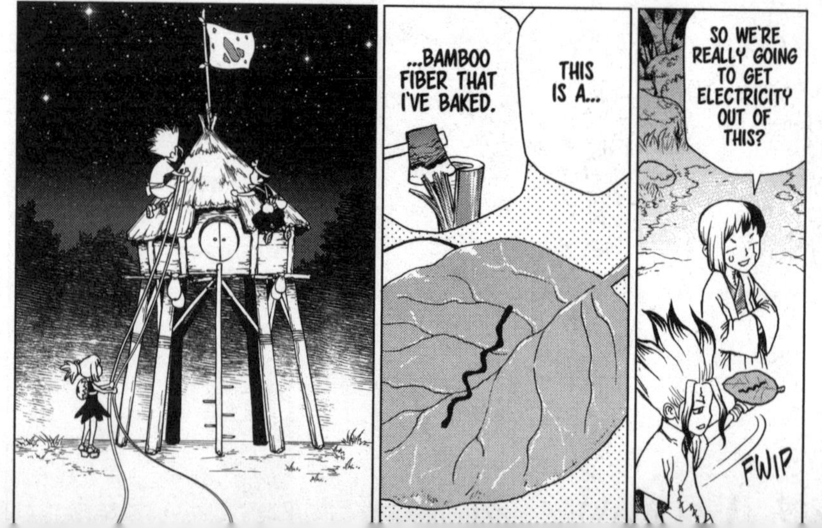
SO WE'RE REALLY GOING TO GET ELECTRICITY OUT OF THIS?
FWIP
THIS IS A...
...BAMBOO FIBER THAT I'VE BAKED.

DOES IT NEED TO BE THAT HIGH UP?
HEH HEH HEH... NOT REALLY. I JUST FIGURE, WHY NOT?
?
WHAT'S HE UP TO?

FREEZE

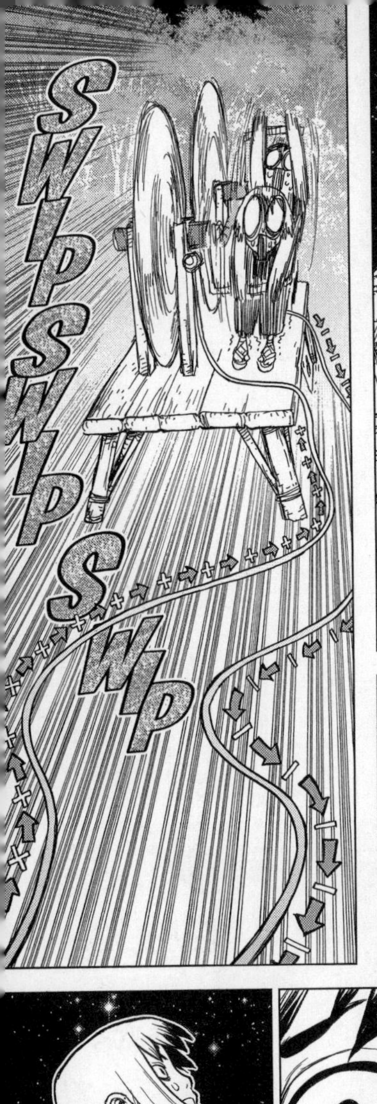
SWIPSWIP
SWP

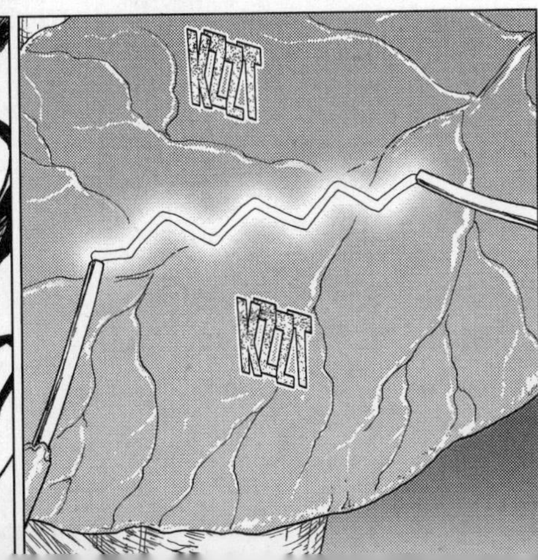
KZZT
KZZT

AH...

OF COURSE.
EDISON!

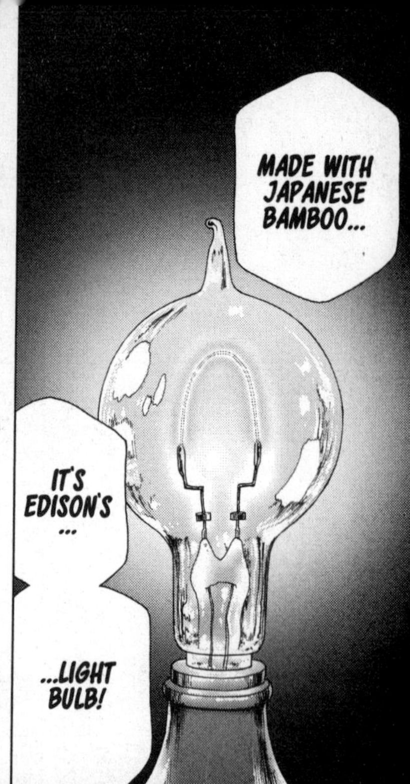
MADE WITH JAPANESE BAMBOO...
IT'S EDISON'S ...
...LIGHT BULB!

CHROME. Y'THINK NIGHTTIME IS SCARY?
WELL, YEAH. CUZ IT GETS ALL DARK.
WHAT'S THAT GOT TO DO WITH IT?

IN OUR DAYS...
...THERE WAS NO DARKNESS.

LIGHT BULBS ERADICATED DARKNESS ALL OVER THE WORLD.
WITH OLD MAN EDISON'S INCANDESCENT BULB...
...WE CONQUERED ALL 24 HOURS OF THE DAY.

WITH THE POWER OF SCIENCE...
...HUMANITY TRIUMPHED OVER THE DARK.
THIS LIGHT...
...FOR THE FIRST TIME IN 3,700 YEARS...
...THOUGH IT DIDN'T EVEN LAST A SECOND...
...BURNED FORTH LIKE NO FIRE EVER COULD.
THE BRIGHT, WHITE...
...LIGHT OF SCIENCE.

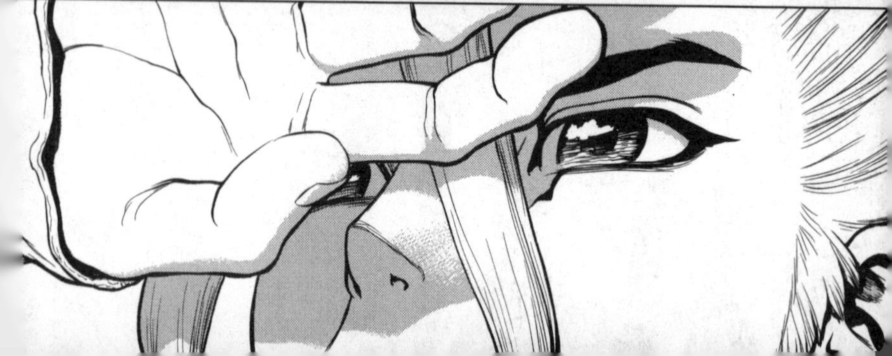

ELEC-TRICITY IN THE STONE AGE?
HARD TO ELIEVE-BAY.

I WONDER IF YOU'RE SEEING THIS...
TSUKASA.

WHEN I STARTED SIFTING THROUGH SCIENCE BOOKS...
...IT WAS THE FIRST BIOGRAPHY I EVER READ.

EDISON'S...
THE LIBRARY WAS TEN BILLION PERCENT GUARANTEED TO HAVE IT, OF COURSE.
Edison
Ohh...
Ohh...
WAIT...SO WHAT THE HECK IS ELECTRICITY?
SO WHEN YOU BREAK IT ALL DOWN, THERE'RE ONLY FOUR KINDS OF FORCES IN THE UNIVERSE?
GRAVITA-TIONAL.
ELECTRO-MAGNETIC... THAT'S ELECTRICITY!!
THEN THE "STRONG FORCE" AND THE "WEAK FORCE"? HEH HEH HEH... SO CRYPTIC I JUST GOTTA LAUGH.
5+3=8

SO IN ALL THE UNIVERSE...
...ELEC-TRICITY'S THE MOST BASIC KINDA POWER THERE IS?
I'M GETTING EXCITED!!

WE'RE GONNA CREATE CIVILIZATION FROM SCRATCH.
WE'LL BE THE ADAM AND EVE...
...OF THIS STONE WORLD.
I WAS REBORN IN THIS PRIMEVAL WORLD...
...NAKED AND ALONE.
AND NOW, ONE YEAR AND FOUR MONTHS LATER...
...I'VE ACHIEVED THIS BASIS OF SCIENCE.
I'VE GOT...
...ELEC-TRICITY.
SHP
I'VE MADE IT. THE FIRST STEP WAS...
...GETTING THIS FAR!!

E=mc²

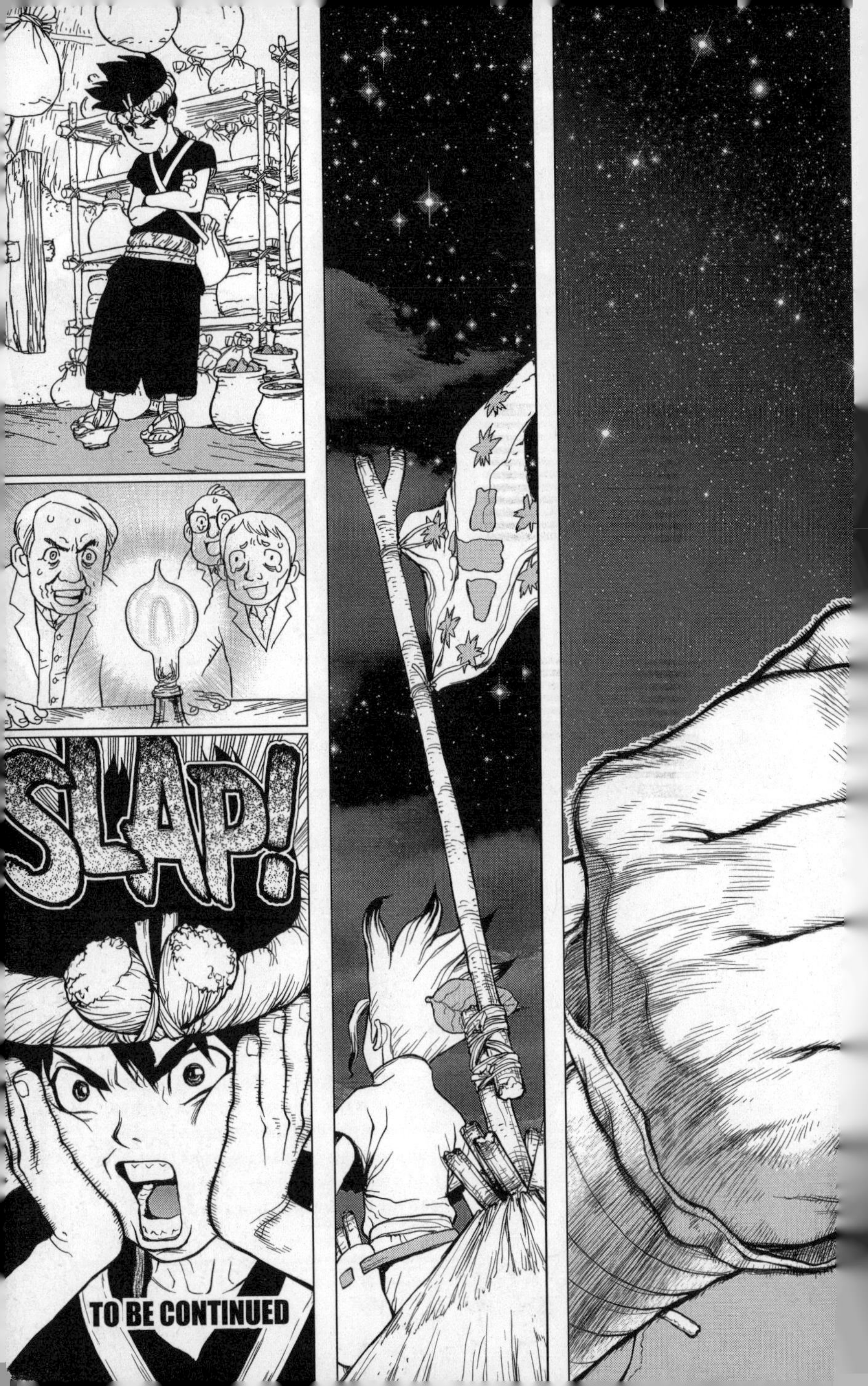
SLAP!
TO BE CONTINUED

YOU'RE READING THE WRONG WAY
Dr.STONE
reads from right to left, starting in the upper-right corner. Japanese is read from right to left, meaning that action, sound effects and word-balloon order are completely reversed from English order.